The Strategy Legacy

The Strategy Legacy

How to Future-Proof a Business and Leave Your Mark

Alex Brueckmann

Leader in applied, concise business books

The Strategy Legacy: How to Future-Proof a Business and Leave Your Mark

Cover design by Alex Brueckmann

Interior design by Exeter Premedia Services Private Ltd., Chennai, India

First published in 2023 by
Business Expert Press, LLC
222 East 46th Street, New York, NY 10017
www.businessexpertpress.com

ISBN-13: 978-1-63742-495-7 (hardcover)
ISBN-13: 978-1-63742-496-4 (paperback)
ISBN-13: 978-1-63742-497-1 (e-book)

Business Expert Press Strategic Management Collection

First edition: 2023

10 9 8 7 6 5 4 3 2 1

In loving memory of Werner Brückmann

THE FIELD GUIDE TO BRING YOUR STRATEGY LEGACY TO LIFE

CREATING THE STRATEGY LEGACY is the field guide to bring your winning strategy to life. The field guide is a companion to The Strategy Legacy and provides all the practical resources and hands-on tools mentioned in the book. Alex Brueckmann shares his proven exercises, checklists, questionnaires, assessments, templates and worksheets. Use this powerful field guide to create the Nine Elements of Organizational Identity and build your strategy legacy.

Scan the code or go to
https://brueckmann.ca/fieldguide for access

Description

A ground-breaking book at the intersection of strategy and leadership! This insightful guide provides a proven process for strategy design combined with the Nine Elements of Organizational Identity framework to align action for success. Whether you're a seasoned executive or a budding entrepreneur, this book is packed with valuable resources, practical illustrations, and humorous cartoons. *The Strategy Legacy* is a must-read to future-proof your organization and become a strategic leader.

Keywords

strategic planning; strategy design; conscious leadership; sustainable business; transformational culture; people-centric growth; leadership development; strategy consulting; purpose-driven practices; values-based business; leading change; disruption mindset

Contents

xii   CONTENTS

Advance Praise

"*Strategy is critical to the success of any business, yet creating a plan, rallying your team behind it, and executing it can feel confusing and overwhelming. Alex's latest book takes the guesswork out of developing a winning strategy in this powerful guide. Full of practical advice and relevant research,* The Strategy Legacy *will leave you equipped and ready to start making a real difference for yourself, your team, and your business today!*"—**Marshall Goldsmith, *New York Times* #1 Bestselling Author**

"*In an age of perpetual disruption and uncertainty, leaders need to rethink strategy.* The Strategy Legacy *provides valuable tools that incorporate identity, purpose, and heart to increase and sustain value creation in the long and short term. And ultimately, because of a broader set of factors and a process of including input throughout the organization, leaders can make a true lasting legacy.*"—**Sanyin Siang, Duke University professor, Thinkers50 #1 Coach and Mentor**

"*The top priority of any business is to create value, and with that comes the need for strategy. Alex Brueckmann has done an excellent job of exploring the critical role of strategy in shaping an organization's identity. This book gives practical advice on how to create a strategy that aligns with an organization's purpose, values, and culture, and how to communicate it effectively.*"—**Hermann Simon, Founder and Honorary Chairman of Simon-Kucher**

"*If you lead people and organizations, or support those that do, then this book is a must-read: full of great insight and providing a clear process to follow. This book will help you find your way to a clarity of purpose and identity that will support you enormously in delivering strategic success. I particularly found that reflection on examples of other organizations' approaches of real interest, inspiring me for my next strategic challenge. This book has given me a framework to make my next strategic journey more organized and efficient, and will make the success probability significantly higher."*—**Richard School-ing, Global Chief Commercial Officer, Alphabet International**

"Having worked in corporate industries for 20-plus years, my unexpected delight at discovering a book that talked to me as though I was in a lively and entertaining strategy workshop was a big surprise. The principles of each topic were then matched by concise theory and reinforced with user-friendly techniques—often humorous examples, made for frequent re-evaluation of my own organization's desired state. I have refreshed much of my thinking on linkages between pillars such as purpose and its anchor to strategy. This book is an excellent blend of theory and application of timeless techniques. I highly recommend this book to anyone, operating at any level, within the working population as there are learnings for all within this book."—**Melanie Vongswang, Chief People Officer, Megaport**

"The Strategy Legacy is a passionate plea to go beyond economic success and growth alone. Can I confidently articulate the magic elements of my strategy? Not sure I give myself a full score on the self-assessment at the end of Part 1. But this is exactly why I enjoyed reading it. This book is a practical do-it-yourself guide for setting up a strategy project. The approach is clearly struc-tured in a framework that Alex explains in a very straightforward way along with examples and tips from his own consulting experience. This book will be helpful for anybody who is defining the strategy for their organization—be it the CEO or Head of Strategy."—**Volker Jacobsen, Managing Director and CEO, Trumpf**

"It's the most important element for the health and long-term success of any organization. And too often, we don't do it well or think it is for others in the company. This book addresses strategy by going beyond how we normally think of it, integrating culture and identity to make strategy personal, and a more noble cause. Rich with examples and research citations, The Strategy Legacy provides a rigorous process that will engage you—and your colleagues—to establish and sustain your strategy. If you care about what you do, and how you do it, and want to bring your colleagues along with you, reading this book is a worthy investment of your time."—**Jim Floberg, Vice President, Roche Diagnostics**

"I've read numerous books on identity, culture, and strategy. While many focus on the WHY and the WHAT only, Alex Brueckmann invites us to also learn about the HOW TO. This book is a captivating read that will leave you inspired to kick off the next strategy process in a more holistic and people-centric way. It is a manual for designing an identity-driven strategy. Alex puts the strategy process as such at the heart of building identity. He equips leaders who care about their organizations' impact with a strategic framework and a detailed guide to harness the hidden power of identity."
—Sebastian Roltsch, Head of Business Operations, Red Bull

"Finally, a book that says it all! Alex captures an often hidden side of a common but often unclear topic, strategy design, and implementation. We are entering an era where people are more connected to their purpose and choose career paths supporting their desired impact. This calls for awareness and action among today's leaders. The Strategy Legacy is brilliant as it helps create your very own roadmap to an impact-driven strategy. A quality not many books offer, and I will surely have the book at hand going forward with my team."—**Helga Johanna Oddsdottir, COO, HS Veitur**

"Have you ever reflected on how to bring strategy in your organization into action? This book provides a fresh and hands-on perspective on strategy in your organization. With many real-life examples, it is your practical guide to understanding strategy beyond its academic concepts. It is an engaging collection of insights and a must-read for anyone who wants to understand the extraordinary relevance of people and organizational identity in any successful strategy process."—**Dr. Markus Schramm, Managing Director, Check24**

"I highly recommend this book to those who want to take more ownership of strategy, who believe in sustainable change, and who want to shape the future as a team, carrying strategy from a boardroom discussion into action across corporate functions. The Nine Elements of Organizational Identity introduced in this book are a truly practical framework. Before reading this book, I never thought so deeply about the role of the organizational identity in building a high-performing organization, fully aligned on all key aspects of their existence: people-centric, purpose-driven, and values-based, anchored in capability building and management systems. The book provides a comprehensive

guide to designing and implementing strategy, combining a hands-on process with inspiring examples. Some highlights I found very useful are the detailed toolbox on the identity design process as well as the six capabilities for implementing organizational identity."—**Dr. Niels Neudecker, Senior Vice President, Kantar**

"*This book is indispensable for practitioners in organizations of any kind who want to lead strategy without necessarily having to rely on external consultants. The process of creating organizational identity is beautifully captured and truly hands-on, underpinned with practical tools. Every step is clearly outlined, the respective goals, value, and end products are well described. I especially enjoyed the framework of the Nine Elements of Organizational Identity because its importance in real life becomes immediately obvious. I hope to read more about each of those elements, maybe in subsequent books or articles addressing each element in even greater detail. Even though the book is packed with valuable content it is easy to follow.*"—**Martin Kewitsch, Executive Vice President, Bertelsmann**

"*This book is a rare find, bringing clarity to the often fuzzy concepts that make up business strategy as a vehicle to deliver organizational identity. Alex has written a leadership book with resources and techniques everyone can put into practice. As I read the book, I often found myself sharing the nuggets I encountered with my business partner, usually with a comment like 'here's something we can use!' Alex writes with intelligence, passion, and humor, interconnecting his points with a combination of intuitive visuals, relevant anecdotes, and practical resources, interspersed with some poignant cartoons. I discovered essential tools I could have used in my past as a CEO of fintech startups. The Strategy Legacy has already found a prominent place on my physical and digital bookshelves, kept within easy reach for constant reference.*"—**Mark Notten, Managing Partner, Silver Peak Associates**

"*With this book, Alex has created a comprehensive strategy manual. It combines a stringent framework with academic research and practical advice. It is loaded with examples, both public and from his extensive experience that illustrate the concepts and highlights pitfalls and challenges. The book provides a framework so clear that anyone—even without strategy experience—can pick it up and get to work. I particularly enjoyed Alex's focus on the people aspect. The best strategic plan cannot succeed if it does not become ingrained in an organization as a North Star to guide people."*—**Kai Roemmelt, Executive Vice President, Best Merchant Partners**

"In a refreshing departure from 'cookie cutter' strategy books, Alex Brueckmann blends his corporate expertise and consulting experience to stitch together nine core facets of organizational identity. Throughout, he manages to avoid cliché, deftly weaving real-world experience with insightful wisdom, supported by practical examples. Without spoiling the surprise, in the dozens of strategy books I've read, I've never found one that so skillfully provides guidance to piece together the inspirational and aspirational with the quantitative measures and control to really align an organization's identity. This book is for anyone running a strategy process—whether that be 'top level' CEO and team—or a regional, divisional, or even functional leader with their respective teams. Trust the book and reap the benefits. Highly recommended."
—**Peter Slack, Executive Vice President Operations, Handicare Group**

"The Strategy Legacy is the book to prepare your business and yourself for the future. Especially for people like me—not born as a natural strategist—the pragmatic connections between impact, strategy, tangible targets, and relevant skills are insightful. This helps to create value for our customers and people, for management, peers, as well as teams. Parts of these concepts we tried out a couple of years ago very successfully. The framework developed into a complete identity design process, mature, pressure tested and easy to implement. It triggered a lot of ideas about unleashing the potential of the organization and inspired me to restart the identity process immediately."—**Jens Wöhler, Head of Global Customer Support, Roche Diagnostics**

"Alex Brueckmann created a wonderful must-read step-by-step guide for senior business executives and strategy leaders. It helps them navigate the complexities that arise while they think about undertaking a strategy and organizational identity exercise. He provides practical illustrations from the real world as to how strategy needs to be anchored to not only help shape the future of an organization but help deliver long-term value to stakeholders beyond just financial gains. I especially like the section where he writes about

organizations that combine strategy and purpose to create a powerful meaning and direction, which bring together leaders, employees, and shareholders, to drive the organization to deliver lasting impact both financially and within society."—**Ankush Bhandari, Entrepreneur and Business Advisor**

"Our people set priorities, make decisions, and do the hard work of achieving results together—strategy in action. When these strategic workflows are driven by a shared purpose, the workplace comes to life fully, and a distinct organizational identity is created. It's a special thing to be a part of. Alex shows us how to unify a company's most essential elements and enable its people with the capabilities necessary for turning great strategy into reality. As Alex writes: strategy is what an organization expects from a leader."—**Daimen Hardie, Cofounder and Executive Director, Community Forests International**

"A highly recommended read for any manager or leader looking to reinvigorate their passion for strategy! In a world where strategy has too often become just another buzzword—misused, abused, and generally watered down—Alex's new book restores clarity and precision to the term. Reading through the Nine Elements of Organizational Identity, you discover a practical framework for developing a high-performing organization. Illustrated by helpful and vivid examples Alex's accessible approach reaches far beyond strategy as a profit maximizer, to bring out the human side of strategy anchored in the organization's culture."—**Edward Boon, Author of *Improving Performance Through Learning***

"While many practitioner books focus on strategy only, this book goes one step beyond and presents a step-by-step manual on how to develop an entire organizational identity. I found the practical examples very illustrative and—as a leader in our organization—resonated a lot with the opportunities and challenges described in running such a process. Reading this page-turner made me want to try out some of the concepts immediately. One chapter that struck me as particularly interesting explores how we can develop the right capabilities in organizations. I highly recommend this book to business leaders, no matter if you are a department head or a C-level executive, as it makes you think about strategy in a more holistic way."—**Stevan Lutz, Chief Financial Officer, HomeToGo**

"With his innovative Nine Elements framework, Alex Brueckmann brings together traditional elements like mission and values and fuses it with critical implementation components like principles and management systems. Most importantly, he provides a map for implementing strategy. The book presents some powerful thoughts on change management, which any good strategy will inspire. This part is often overlooked and ignored by consultants and organizations and leads to good strategies collecting dust. Most books and essays tackle the components of strategy like a jigsaw, one at a time, which don't intuitively fit together at first glance. I know now how to make the pieces of the jigsaw fit."—**Martin Rydlo, Vice President, Overnight Recovery Brands**

"This book truly helps you define what your organization stands for. I recommend reading this book whether you are a young professional, a serial entrepreneur, or an experienced corporate leader. What I admire is Alex's view that great leaders are more than profit-driven but instead combine business and people focus, based on a clear moral compass. A fun and easy read, the book guides you through the jungle of strategic challenges in today's fast-paced business environment. Alex provides us with hands-on tools to craft organizational identity and strategy. He merges his professional experience with academic frameworks and discusses the challenges and success stories of well-known organizations."—**Ekaterina Bozoukova, Cofounder and CEO, Womire**

"Along with a comprehensive and well-structured strategy process, the book dives deep into the steps of strategy development. The Strategy Legacy invites us to shape strategy and challenge the status quo. It provides helpful methods that all of us can add to our toolbox, supporting us while we drive change. Easy to read, quick to grasp—just like a good strategy!"—**Constantin Doenges, Director Strategy and Transformation, Fresenius Kabi**

Acknowledgments

This book would first and foremost not be possible without the privilege I've had to work with inspiring leaders and entrepreneurs. Over the years, some of these relationships have developed into friendships. I sincerely appreciate the privilege of collaborating with you and your teams. Thank you for trusting me and allowing me to help you build a legacy you love.

In all this, I couldn't have succeeded alone. To the many amazing coaches, facilitators, trainers, and colleagues I met along the way: Thank you for your friendship and collaboration!

A special thanks goes to those involved during the writing process. Without your guidance, I might have written an entirely different book, undoubtedly not a better one. Your feedback helped me balance the content and make it as rich as possible.

Sam Hiyate of The Rights Factory, you believed in the book from Day 1. You advocated for it, and you helped me to see the grand scheme of things in the book publishing world. Thank you for being the best literary agent I could ask for.

Everyone at Business Expert Press Publishing: Thank you for helping this book see the light of day: Prof. John A. Pearce II, Scott Isenberg, Charlene Kronstedt, Melissa Yeager, Sung Tinnie.

Rystana Petrovsky, my favorite editor. I'm in awe experiencing your ability to condense information into content that feels like a full meal. You inspire me to become a better writer, and I can't wait to work with you again. Thank you for making editing this book a joy ride!

Lori Ames, Jenna Mallimo, and Christina Czachor at ThePRFreelancer, Inc.: Thank you for being my public relations dream team! I value your positivity and the ease of collaborating with you. A shared set of values can make all the difference.

A very special thanks goes to my family. Stephanie and Caelum, your encouragement made me start and eventually complete this book. Thank you for the love you bring into our lives.

Introduction

Why I Wrote This—and Whom
It Is For

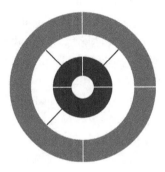

One morning, one of the richest business people of his time opens the newspaper, shocked to read about his own death. While it was his brother who died, the reporter falsely wrote the obituary about him. The headline calls attention, *The Merchant of Death is dead*. The obituary shatters his self-image of being a benefactor for humankind. The businessman is successful by many people's standards, especially from a financial standpoint. But now he realizes he has not lived a life of significance. He decides to work toward a legacy he can be proud of and sets a powerful will in motion.

What is the living legacy *you* are building? Does success or significance guide the way you lead? How do you want to be remembered when you move on to your next adventure? You will leave a legacy, whether you want to or not. Legacy is like culture—every person and every organization has one. It is consciously honed over time into a secret sauce that distinguishes you from competitors. It may even come to life subconsciously or by accident. Maybe it falls somewhere in between.

Leaders and entrepreneurs have a threefold responsibility, including the people they lead, the organization they represent, and society. I call this the Legacy Trident. A living legacy can reflect all three perspectives simultaneously. You might be an incredible talent developer and lead with a positive legacy. However, senior management might only see that you've repeatedly missed performance targets, forming a negative reputation. Finally, society might see your organization as a destroyer of nature, rather than a company mining for precious metals. Your focus in these three areas may vary; some might care more about their legacy, while others focus on the bigger picture of the business they're leading.

The first spike of the Legacy Trident is your legacy as a leader. Building a positive legacy first requires self-reflection to achieve self-awareness and to overcome blind spots, ego, and biases. Developing a crystal-clear moral compass guides our decision making based on ethical grounds. Once our moral compass is in place, we can bring it to work. Let's be human! By benchmarking business-related decisions against our ethical system, we start building toward a better legacy. Naturally, people perceive leaders as inspirational and influential if they follow a clear set of values. As a result, they follow your example and make better decisions themselves. To positively impact others, you must start by looking internally, and it will stem from there.

The second tip of the trident represents your legacy as a creator of culture for your organization. By emulating your behaviors, those around you become multipliers of your legacy, creating a ripple effect through-out an organization, and spilling over into their personal lives. Shaping a more conscious culture is an essential contribution to your organization. You have a choice—live up to your moral obligation and take care of those you lead. Coach them, mentor them, and help them become the best version of themselves. Even if your organization's incentive structure rewards financial performance over developing people or leading based on a moral compass, you can still choose to change structures, remove barriers, and build a people-centric legacy. Push the first domino to create a beautiful chain reaction.

The third spike of the Legacy Trident is the legacy a business leaves by making the world a better place. If this sounds too grand, think of *community* instead of *world* to become a true force for change. We must overcome old paradigms like shareholder value and establish a socially and environmentally responsible organizational concept. Leaders must harness the power of organizational identity to build better businesses and create a more equitable world.

If you take stock right now, what's the living legacy you are building? Is it a positive one, or a legacy you'd rather escape?

Shocked by his obituary, the businessman from the beginning of our story was jolted into action. When he died eight years later, he left his fortune to a fund that rewards the people who have conferred the greatest benefit to humankind in the previous year. By now, you have probably figured out who that man was. Alfred Nobel, the inventor of nitroglycerin and dynamite, who became the founder of the Nobel prize. To this day, Nobel laureates receive awards financed by the interest of Alfred Nobel's fortune. A truly remarkable turnaround into a legacy that continues to do good long after his passing.

For many of us, care for the future is the driving force behind taking charge and shaping the way forward. Caring is about making conscious, clear decisions, and about defining direction. For businesses, clarity and direction are often associated with terms like purpose, vision, or strategy. I first got in touch with these terms in business school and did not find the subject of strategy very appealing, to say the least. In the setting where I was learning it, the subject lacked relevance because it had no visible connection to my preuniversity career as a content creator in the media industry. I couldn't see it back then, but strategy has since become the biggest passion in my career.

My own life reflects the power of strategy. I grew up in the 1980s and early 1990s, in a small rural village in Germany, and I never felt that I fit in. As long as I remember, I wanted to escape what I perceived as a change-averse environment, which was stifling my creativity and personal expression. But I didn't know how to do it outside of my imagination. I didn't have a well-planned strategy in place. Pursuing my dreams, I searched for ways to become who I aspired to be. At the age of 23, I realized I was hitting a glass ceiling in my career development and decided to go back to the drawing board. In hindsight, this was the moment I became strategic about my life.

I had developed a clear picture of how I wanted my life to look. I knew I had to prioritize a few things in life above everything else. I decided to return to school full-time, earning the credentials needed to enter university. When it was time to choose a discipline, I decided against subjects I first felt were obvious choices. I didn't ask myself where my passion lied, but which domain would provide the most diverse opportunities for my work life. Willing to pick a field of study I initially didn't connect with emotionally, I chose General Management. I chewed my way through a mountain of dry matter, knowing that I'd rather suffer through a few years and enjoy decades of fulfilling work later. In the end, it paid off. After graduating from the European Business School, strategy became my one true passion in business and life.

The idea for this book came in the aftermath of what I call a self-induced external shock. When my spouse and I decided to relocate from Germany to Canada, the excitement dragged with it an unanticipated aftertaste. I felt strangely guilty about leaving my clients in Europe behind, even if I was moving closer to those in North America. I started talking about this feeling, and a friend joked, "maybe you want to thank your clients and hand them a nice farewell present?" We had a hearty laugh—as if it was so simple.

In the back of my head, the idea of a present developed further. Ultimately, I concluded that my experience designing and implementing organizational identity would be worth sharing. This book is for those who want to improve lives and build toward a better future, whether you are a corporate leader, an entrepreneur, or a startup founder. I want to inspire you to make strategy and organizational identity your thing. I have embedded the topic of strategy in a framework I'll soon introduce to you as the *Nine Elements of Organizational Identity*. You will discover the hidden power of strategy, beyond the context of profit maximization, and in the light of people, impact, values, and strategic capability building.

The Nine Elements of Organizational Identity is not a shiny new strategy tool or the latest theory. This book was written by a practitioner, for practitioners. Anchored in countless projects, forged in the trenches of business reality, I developed, tested, and enhanced this framework over almost two decades, with large and small businesses globally. These companies are among some of the most successful in their fields. In other words, it works and delivers results.

After reading this book, you will be able to properly run a strategy and identity process, leading to more clarity and direction than ever before.

You will know which desirable factors to focus on, which unwanted side effects to avoid, and how to anchor strategy and identity in your business to make them stick. A true legacy.

Per definition, this book is a work in progress, and I don't have all the answers. Still, as I'm striving for excellence, not perfection, I want to share what I've found up until now. My goal is to help you take action, by decoupling the topic of strategy from boardrooms and the metaphorical ivory towers of corporate functions.

I would like to entice you to approach strategy by combining commercial and cultural aspects, and I invite you to put strategy at the heart of your organization's identity. We will talk about why—unfortunately— no one cares about your purpose (as much as you do) and how creating tangible impact helps you build a legacy.

You will embrace JOMO, abundance, growth, and speed as the optimal mindsets of strategic leaders. You will learn a lesson from my former football coach that hopefully inspires you to turn strategy into everyone's business. You will discover six critical skills that you will stop calling *soft*. And finally, you will explore what architecture indicates about avoiding the symphony of destruction and building a support structure to deflect a wrecking ball from knocking down your business.

I will help you simultaneously understand strategy as a driver of corporate culture and commercial success. A people-centric strategy becomes your vehicle to deliver identity and culture, resulting in lasting success for your organization.

Strategy empowers. It is a set of key priorities that form a framework for decision making. When an opportunity presents itself, we benchmark it against that framework. We make intentional choices that propel us closer to the desired future. We say *yes* to things that support our dreams. We stop caring about other businesses' tactics. We start distinguishing shiny objects from real opportunities, fake from value, and stop hustling without direction. A strategy allows us to lead the life we want. As a result, our actions become focused and aligned with our values. We start building toward a legacy that inspires ourselves and those around us.

PART 1

Understanding Identity and the Central Role of Strategy

Serial entrepreneur, Sir Richard Branson famously said about business, "Screw it, just do it and get on and try it." Branson certainly has made some significant business decisions in his life. However, I suggest that a *screw it, just do it* attitude is the opposite of having a solid strategy. Every corporate leader, entrepreneur, and business owner must face the topic of strategy at some point. It's what an organization expects from a leader. Great leaders recognize the potential of strategy processes and see that they hold the power to create more than just strategy. It is the best opportunity to rally an organization around an identity beyond its commercial future.

If you've ever been involved in building a strategy, you have likely experienced how resource-consuming such a process can be. A strategy process often involves a significant number of contributors, requiring additional work from those in an organization already at max capacity. Ask yourself how often you should approach these individuals with some sort of on-top or side gig, before they become annoyed or unwilling to support these efforts. You want to involve your people as much as possible and as carefully as possible simultaneously. Therefore, a strategy process is the best opportunity for leaders to define all elements of organizational identity in one relentless effort, not just the strategy piece.

In the first part of this book, I will introduce organizational identity based on my experience from over 20 years in the corporate and consulting world. I blend real-life examples and academic research into an actionable framework called the Nine Elements of Organizational Identity. It will be your guide to identity design and execution, holistically and sustainably. These nine elements will help remove any dangerously narrow and short-term thinking from your business approach. As a result, you can create a business strategy anchored in your organization's culture and translate it into a clear implementation path.

CHAPTER 1

Making New Friends

The Nine Elements of Organizational Identity

A company's identity encapsulates what it takes to build a fully aligned and high-performing organization. This alignment brings clarity and synchronizes your organization to enable everyone to focus in the same direction. Imagine the speed and impact your organization could have if you reached this level of clarity! But why would an organization need an identity in the first place?

I suggest the number of people searching for meaning, impact, and belonging has never been higher than today. There is a drive to seek out identity more extremely than before. We join monks for meditation, go on long pilgrimages to reconnect with body and soul, and try to live a more grounded life. Some of us desperately try to liberate ourselves from the never-ending rat race for more money, status, and mind-numbing consumerism.

I have witnessed businesses become more than transactional partners for money and status. These organizations are great places to work, where individuals are valued for their contributions. Companies have the power to provide meaning and a sense of belonging to their employees—yet many are simply not leveraging this opportunity. The term corporate citizenship comes to mind, referring to an organization's role in the broader community, acting responsibly, and propelling society rather than just increasing shareholder value.

Once we explore profound questions about our existence, these thoughts stick like chewing gum on sneaker soles. Searching for answers, people crave new kinds of incentives, benefits, and motivations from their workplaces. Organizations answer by providing more purposeful work and changing their leadership culture away from commanding top-down.

I dare to say that The Great Resignation of 2022 was just the beginning. Businesses need to prepare themselves for the storm that will sweep talent either into or out of organizations, depending on whether they can provide meaning and belonging. Leaders should embrace the power of organizational identity to create places of work that deliver value beyond money.

The Nine Elements of Organizational Identity are structured in three circles. The inner circle of impact, mission, and principles forms the foundation of who you are as a business. What do you do, and for whom? Why are you doing it, and what is the tangible impact you create? Which values guide your actions? The middle circle is the strategic core of your identity. What will your business look like in a few years from now? What are your strategic priorities to achieve that vision? What are the key goals

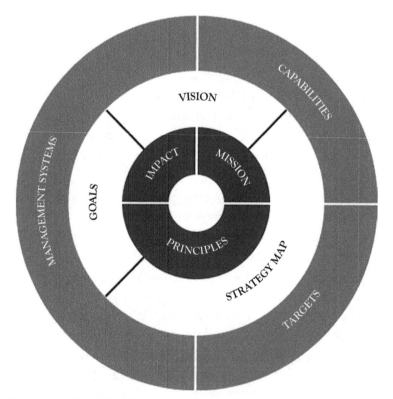

Figure 1.1 The Nine Elements of Organizational Identity

you will reach? The outer circle enables your organization to put strategy into action and live up to your identity. What do we need to learn? How do we enable and empower action? How do we anchor transformation?

These broad terms and words may, at first, beg many questions, which I hope to answer by the end of this book. Some of these elements are particularly tangible, and they may exist in your organization already, perhaps management systems, for example. You may have encountered some of them in your career, like mission and principles. Other elements, such as impact, might be less commonly in place.

You might already be familiar with organizational identity as a field of study within the discipline of organizational theory. Academic theorists suggest that it could take years for organizations to see the results of their efforts. I will not discuss academic theory as such in this book. Neither will I link my framework to organizational theory. The Nine Elements of Organizational Identity is a practical framework, grounded in projects I have completed with clients. The approach described in this book will help you rerail your organization on a path that yields results—within a significantly shorter time than theorists might suggest. Let's explore the nine elements.

Impact is the change you want to create based on your purpose (your reason to exist as an organization).

Function: It creates orientation, credibility, and legitimization.

Characteristics: It is tangible and turns your intention (purpose) into visible results.

The first element of identity is *impact*. It translates purpose into action and fuels your fire. Impact and purpose motivate employees and other stakeholders to perform at their best daily. Their focus is less on financial success and more on building a business and life of significance. The purpose is the reason an organization matters, and it should go beyond money, status, or other transactional factors. It should be more than increasing the wealth of shareholders or paying salaries to employees. The impact is your visible contribution to society, for example, preserving nature.

Impact and purpose address a good cause and are grand and idealistic. It is no wonder that not-for-profit organizations (NPOs) often have the most potent and powerful purpose statements, often closely linked to their visible impact:

- Environment protection organizations: *to protect wildlife and preserve natural resources and habitat*
- Food banks and hunger-relief charities: *to collect and distribute food helping people struggling with hunger*
- UNHCR—The United Nations High Commissioner for Refugees: *to safeguard the rights and well-being of refugees*

Organizations must take accountability for their intentions and translate purpose into impact. For this reason, I have labeled this element *impact*, instead of purpose.

Principles are underlying values and behavioral guidelines.

Function: They provide a framework for collaboration and behaviors.

Characteristics: They are non-negotiable and universally valid within an organization.

With the desired impact in place, organizations can inform their *principles*, the second element of identity. Principles are a set of nonnegotiable values that guide desired behaviors, universally valid for every individual in an organization. They are an essential building block of an organization's desired culture. A great example of values brought to life is the American outdoor apparel and gear company, Patagonia. Their four core values[1] follow one theme: protecting the planet:

- *Build the best product*: Their focus is on function, repairability, and durability. The longer a product lasts, the better for the planet.
- *Cause no unnecessary harm*: They recognize that operating a business is causing an ecological footprint, and they are working to reduce it.

- *Use business to protect nature*: Patagonia, as a business, is dedicated to protecting the planet.
- *Not bound by convention:* The company is constantly searching for new ways to do things, both operationally and strategically.

Over the decades, Patagonia has reached a reputation for putting its money where its mouth is. They have pledged 1 percent of their sales to grassroots environmental nonprofits, to support nature preservation and restoration.

Putting values into action doesn't require millions of dollars. During a heatwave in the Summer of 2021, Patina Brewing, a local craft brewery in Port Coquitlam, Canada, filled its core value *community* with life. Unlike many homes and apartments, their pub was lucky to have air-conditioning. Outside of business hours, the brewery didn't serve drinks or food, but opened its doors for people to have a cool place to work.[2]

Besides values, behavioral guidelines are also a part of principles. Behavioral guidelines outline the desired comportment of everyone in an organization. For example, they capture how teams should collaborate, or how leaders should treat associates and other stakeholder groups.

Mission is what an organization aims to do, and for whom.

Function: It defines an organization's field of activity or business.

Characteristics: No frills.

Let's talk about the third element of identity, a *mission*. It should be a plain explanation of what an organization does and for whom, a simple phrase everyone can understand. A great example is the Sea Shepherd Conservation Society, "Our mission is to protect defenseless marine wildlife and end the destruction of habitat in the world's oceans."[3] Plain and simple. One of the best statements I have come across describes the mission of the voluntary fire brigades in Germany. They use just four verbs: *save, extinguish, rescue, protect*—people, animals, and material assets, in this order. I have difficulty imagining a more precise explanation of what they do and for whom.

Vision can best be defined as an organization's desired state sometime in the future.

Function: It paints a picture that engages and motivates people.

Characteristics: It addresses the hearts and minds of key stakeholder groups.

The fourth element of identity is *vision*. According to researchers Sooksan Kantabutra and Gayle Avery, some commonly shared characteristics of powerful visions are conciseness, clarity, future orientation, stability, challenge, abstractness, and desirability or ability to inspire.[4]

The challenge is to formulate a vision that contains both the details of an organization's picture of the future and is still memorable. The vision of Wikipedia is short, memorable, precise, and for those contributing to the community, it is truly inspirational. "Imagine a world in which every single person on the planet is given free access to the sum of all human knowledge. That's what we're doing."[5] Later in the book, I will dissect Wikipedia's vision statement to explore which characteristics make for a strong vision statement: solid and magical while simultaneously specific enough to provide guidance and inspire action. Without solidifying your vision, it will remain an illusion.

Strategy maps visually depict an organization's strategic priorities.

Function: They steer the organization toward the vision.

Characteristics: They address different stakeholder perspectives along the value chain.

Let's talk about the fifth element of identity, *strategy maps*. They capture what an organization aims to accomplish and the clear-cut priorities that will do the job. A strategy map helps an organization maneuver toward its vision, just like an explorer would use a geographic map to navigate in unknown territory toward a destination.

Management thinkers Robert Kaplan and David Norton introduced strategy maps to visualize an organization's objectives according to their impact on financial performance, customers, internal business processes, and learning and growth.[6]

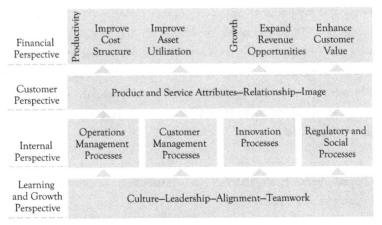

Figure 1.2 Strategy map, adapted from Kaplan and Norton

Kaplan and Norton's work has been inspiring the approach to strategy design of leaders, scholars, and management consultants. The tool has been merged with and integrated into new ideas and concepts and is applied in various ways today. I will provide an example in Chapter 6, where I describe the content and flow of a strategy workshop.

I appreciate that there are other tools available to capture a strategy. I suggest strategy maps as a tool of choice because they feel relatively intuitive, even if a team has little experience using such tools. If you are more familiar with other strategy tools, providing similarly actionable results, stick to those tools.

Goals are the operational breakdown of strategy.

Function: They help move strategy into action.

Characteristics: They are specific, measurable, action-oriented, realistic, and time-bound (SMART), the basis for individual targets.

I often find leadership teams refer to *strategy* as the combination of a vision and strategy map. Besides an inspiring vision and a detailed strategy map, one more element usually belongs to a strategy: *goals*—the sixth element of identity.

Organizations fill strategy maps with concrete projects to make their initiative graspable and bring it to life. Depending on the scope of a strategy and the size of an organization, they cluster various projects into workstreams. These are closely linked to an organization's operational business to translate strategy into action. And exactly here would we find goals. Goals measure how successfully we implement workstreams. They sit between strategic key performance indicators (KPIs) measuring the vision, and the more operational KPIs tracking the progress of projects within a workstream.

Targets describe an individual's contribution to implementing organizational identity.

Function: They create transparency, motivate, and make contribution matter.

Characteristics: They are role-specific, addressing several elements of identity.

After filling workstreams with goals and projects, you must take one final step to bring strategic priorities to life. The seventh element of identity involves breaking goals down into individual *targets* for each contributor. It's simple: no targets, no implementation because, in the end, organizations don't bring organizational identity to life—people do, by contributing their share. While targets make strategy relevant to everyone's day-to-day job, they must reflect more than only strategic goals. Targets create role-specific transparency about an individual's contribution to implementing all identity elements.

Figure 1.3 Hierarchy of measurement criteria

Capabilities are mission-critical skills for implementing organizational identity.

Function: They enable people to cope with change and live up to expectations.

Characteristics: They include occupational skills and a specific set of interpersonal skills.

Capabilities are the eighth element of identity. Making organizational identity relevant to everyone in an organization is one of the trickiest pieces during implementation. To master this challenge, organizations must invest in building the related capabilities as a part of any identity process; it prevents a strategy from failing to deliver the expected results.

Unfortunately, I have seen leaders struggle to load their team's day-to-day activities with strategic relevance. If leaders cannot create this link, individuals can't connect with identity emotionally or rationally. This is true, especially for those sitting far from senior leadership, leaving them unclear about their role in implementing the strategy. Consequently, entire groups of an organization's population may feel that these topics are *for those up there*, meaning senior leaders and others involved in the design process, not for them.

Organizations shouldn't stop at the leadership level when it comes to learning and capability development. Sure, leaders are key multipliers, they are not the only ones, though. As a new identity brings change, enable your people to perform at their best and find satisfaction in their roles by equipping them with the essential competencies.

Management systems are frameworks to steer an organization.

Function: They help achieve strategic and operational objectives.

Characteristics: They support the status quo, not the change, and need to be adjusted.

New strategies invariably push organizations into unchartered territory. If that's not the case, what's the point of a new strategy in the first place? Let's assume an organization has done a great job defining their strategy and implementation is well under way. When does an organization know that it has mastered all aspects of change and strategy execution? *Management systems* are useful indicators; they are the ninth element of organizational identity.

Management systems are the processes, policies, and procedures that help steer an organization. These systems are designed to keep an organization stable. To ensure that these systems support the execution of a new strategy rather than hinder it, organizations need to adjust their management systems, like remuneration and incentive structure. Needless to say, it should reward desired behaviors and performance in line with an organization's identity, rather than keeping people from embracing it. How rigorously leadership adjusts management systems is an indicator of how sticky a new identity will be.

CHAPTER 2

No One Cares About Purpose

Creating Impact and a Living Legacy

Economist Milton Friedman's widely applied notion that an organization's greatest responsibility is to serve their shareholders and to maximize profits seems to be dying.* By contrast, a fundamentally new understanding of the role of organizations emerges. In 2019, the Business Roundtable, a group of CEOs of major U.S. corporations issued a statement on *The Purpose of a Corporation.*[1] Over 200 corporate leaders signed the bill, including Amazon's Jeff Bezos, BlackRock's Laurence Fink, Microsoft's Satya Nadella, and Goldman Sachs's David Solomon. The statement acknowledges that, while each company serves its own corporate purpose, they also share a fundamental commitment to all stakeholders: customers, employees, suppliers, communities and the environment, and shareholders. This statement is certainly a step in the right direction. But businesses can do much more than manifest their intentions.

A Purpose Is Just an Intent

The danger of stopping at *why* is that you miss out on creating a deeper impact. Consumers, employees, and investors can tell whether you are serious about turning your purpose into action, or if you are falling behind the expectations you raised. Organizations that combine strategy and impact into something powerful provide meaning and direction to leaders, employees, and shareholders. An organization's reason for

---

* M. Friedman. 1912–2006. American Nobel Prize Winner in Economic Sciences.

existence needs to be more than just platitudes: it should legitimize you and must go way beyond making money or securing jobs.

Unfortunately, the concept of *purpose* has degenerated into a buzz-word. Even if businesses define their purpose well, they often don't do anything at all to fulfill it.[2] Or worse: as a polished veneer wrapped around a less noble core, purpose statements sometimes try to swathe talent, investors, and the public.

The Coca-Cola Company's purpose statement reads, "Refresh the world. Make a difference." The company has been partnering with the World Wild-life Fund (WWF) since 2007 in water stewardship, "To help ensure healthy, thriving freshwater basins around the world," as it reads on the company website. At the same time, Coca-Cola has been accused of zero progress on reducing plastic waste, after repeatedly being named the world's top plastic polluter. In no way do I want to diminish the company's efforts with the WWF. But can they credibly claim that they are making a difference at scale?

In a recent conversation I had with author and management consultant Ron Carucci, he said about purpose statements:

> Earn your right to write them down. Have a sense for what they are, and go model them, let people notice them, let people be able to infer them. If you write them down before you've earned your right, they become weaponized. People hold them up as a yardstick to say, "you're not doing this."

Purpose has many complex layers of meaning, which may or may not resonate with every individual in a certain organization. This begs the question: if an organization's purpose doesn't resonate with everyone, or measure up to expectations, is it the right concept in the first place, or should we search for an alternative concept that can unite and provide direction in a better way?

It may be hard to hear: in the end, no one cares about your purpose as much as you do. It is an intent—something you aim for, something you want to achieve. The purity of your intent, however, is not enough. Intent doesn't change anything, talking about your purpose is silver. Acting based on your intent to create a positive impact is gold.

In many aspects of our lives, even outside of the workplace, we've gone over a tipping point where talking won't create the change we need.

That's why, people take to the streets and protest for what they believe in more than ever. Black Lives Matter and Fridays for Future result from people being fed up with *the talk*. People need *action* to create a just society and stop the worsening climate emergency. We need companies to do, not intend to do. I suggest we start making an impact rather than stopping at purpose. That's where business strategy comes into play. It should serve to translate your purpose into action.

Employees want to feel that their contributions make a difference and are agents of change rather than idle bystanders. Corporate purpose statements are often just marketing claims, trying to make a company look good at first sight. When you start peeling off the veneer, you realize a different reality. And that is why employees and consumers are fed up with hollow statements.

People no longer settle for an employer who simply switches off lights on Earth Day, or organizes a one-day beach clean-up, or a 10k run to raise awareness and collect funds for a rare disease. Instead, people are looking for jobs that allow them to be wholly committed to a cause that has the power to disrupt their entire life, becoming positive activist employees. Results matter more than intent. That's why, impact is indeed more relevant than purpose.

Tap Into New Business Opportunities
Following Your Why Not

Welcome to the age of the impact investor, the activist employee, the informed consumer. We increasingly hold brands and companies accountable for what they do, and the stand they take during times of social upheaval, political instability, and environmental emergencies. As consumers, we make companies feel the consequences of violating our values when we stop buying their products. As employees, we might be distracted by shiny purpose statements but won't stand for being stuck in a corporate machine that doesn't deliver on its promises. As investors, we don't want dirty money from unprofessionally governed companies that pollute the environment, exploit workers, lie, or allow management to get away with shady behavior.

Finding your purpose matters. Your intent matters. However, and this may seem contrary at first, you shouldn't start with a search for your *why*. You should start by asking: *why not*? *Why not* do the right thing now? *Why not* stop doing the things we aren't benefiting from? *Why not* put people first, profit second? *Why not* use our market position and purchasing power to positively impact social standards, protect the environment, and stand up for a good cause? *Why not* speak up as an organization?

How many resources should you channel toward your *why not*? There is a business case for doing the right thing, where companies tap into new markets, open new revenue streams, and access new consumer groups by changing how they conduct business. One such example, Unilever, grew their profit considerably from Lipton tea after establishing more sustainable environmental and social practices throughout their supply chain. They linked their sustainability efforts to their existing marketing budget and attracted a whole new group of conscious consumers.[3]

The bigger a company, the higher they should aim with their *why not*. The more money a corporation makes, the greater the responsibility to offset its negative impact. Their sustainability and environmental, social, and governance (ESG) practices must reflect how seriously they take their *why not*, rather than seeing ESG practices solely to reduce risk exposure. The size and potential of your *why not* can be considerable.

Consider linking salaries and benefits to a meaningful change and the resulting financial performance rather than to purely financial metrics. I'd love to see CEO salaries tied to doing good, not just doing well. It's important to lead as if your children are watching to build toward a better future.

For the Coca-Cola Company, this could be nothing short of completely surrendering the use of new materials for their packaging and aiming for 100 percent recycled materials. And it doesn't have to stop there: *why not* strive toward carbon neutrality now? *Why not* educate people about the health implications of sugary drinks? *Why not* reconfigure the supply chain based on social and environmental sustainability? *Why not* help establish waste management and recycling systems in countries where plastic bottles are discarded into rivers and washed into the ocean?

It is when we ask *why not* that we allow ourselves to think beyond the obvious to build a living legacy. If you want your intent to be more than just a phrase, you must look beyond money.

At the beginning of the COVID-19 outbreak in 2020, Swiss pharmaceutical company Hoffmann-La Roche lived up to their intent, "Doing now what patients need next." CEO Severin Schwan announced that they had developed a rapid test to diagnose an infection, and that the company would provide the test kits for free to China (at that time, heavily affected by the virus). Commercializing the tests was secondary.[4]

Tapping into business opportunities that support your *why not* is more straightforward than some might think, as the possibilities may come in abundance. For-profit organizations haven't dared enough yet to ask *why not*. Forward-thinking businesses are entering the marketplace, tapping into the vast potential of sustainable entrepreneurship, from circular economy to green energy. They are fast, innovative, and dare to explore and experiment. If you want to do the right thing, you can—the business cases will follow.

For larger organizations, the board of directors plays a crucial role. They might want to nudge their companies in the right direction. Linking executives' salary to impact, rather than financial performance alone, might be an excellent step to establish a stronger *why not*. From there, the company can successfully reshape the business into a future-fit, sustainable organization.

Bringing a Legacy Trident to Life

Why should a reputable company consider reshaping its business approach? Apart from doing the right thing from a sustainability standpoint, it also pays off financially. In its 2021 poll, Axios Harris surveyed close to 43,000 Americans to discover which brands they think to falter or excel in society. Coca-Cola tanked, dropping to 58th and losing 17 ranks from the previous survey.

On the other hand, Patagonia soared from number 32nd all the way to the top of the list because of its unwavering commitment to the environment. They are a shining example of going beyond intent, creating real impact through climate action. Over decades, they've attracted loyal customers, supporting the causes they fight for and growing their bottom line.

Patagonia is an example where an intent translates into meaningful action. Opposingly, Coca-Cola is a classic case of purpose-washing, where words and actions only partly align. Research has found a positive correlation between an organization's sustainability and ESG practices, and financial performance. That means your *why not* yields higher returns. It is as simple as that. So, *why not* turn your company into a force for social and environmental sustainability? *Why not* formulate a grand purpose and translate it into action and impact? Let's dare to stop thinking small.

Become curious, apply a learner's mindset, and be nonjudgmental; you will then be ready to explore the essential questions regarding strategy and impact, as part of your organizational identity. This is a chance to lift your strategy and business to the next level.

In August 2022, Patagonia founder Yvon Chouinard transferred ownership of the U.S.$3 billion company to the new Patagonia Purpose Trust and the Holdfast Collective. He announced that he was here on outdirecting all profits to fight climate change and preserve undeveloped land worldwide. "Earth is now our only shareholder," Chouinard wrote on the company website, and added, "Instead of 'going public,' you could say we're 'going purpose.'"[5] I suspect that the cumulative positive impact Patagonia will create over the next decades will be second to none, because Chouinard didn't stop at *why*. Instead, he built a financially successful business that helped him leave a mark of significance.

Chouinard has been creating an impact through his company for decades. He is famous for his critical stance against capitalism, searching for new ways to reduce the collateral damage, specifically the negative impact that running a business can toll on the planet. Chouinard followed his heart and built a thriving business based on his values—the first spike of the Legacy Trident. More and more talent gravitated toward the company to support its cause, establishing a culture and community of impact—the second spike. Making Earth Patagonia's only shareholder, Chouinard finished the third spike, cementing his legacy toward society and nature for generations to come. Dedicating all profits to environmental protection makes Chouinard's Legacy Trident complete. That's a huge, positive impact.

CHAPTER 3

What's for Breakfast

Strategy and Culture

The world as we know it is transforming. Between 2020 and 2023, we've seen tectonic shifts in the political and economic landscape in which businesses are operating. A global pandemic combined with increasing geopolitical tensions led to supply shortages and soaring inflation. We recognize that we are not doing enough to circumvent catastrophic climate change. Formerly marginalized groups are asserting their seat at the table. The speed of technological advancement is mind-boggling.

While the challenges of a postpandemic era can be frightening, this landscape offers strategic business opportunities. They combine signaling-based crisis response, value-driven strategy, and foresight-informed long-term bets. This creates the basis for a high-performance culture that future-proofs a business as much as humanly possible.

Strategy Between Foresight and Signaling

A business strategy typically addresses a mid-term time horizon of three to five years. Businesses should also explore what lies before and beyond this timeframe. To complement their strategy (mid-term), organizations need foresight (long-term) and signaling (short-term). Signaling addresses the immediate future, and foresight explores what's beyond the planning horizon of the current business strategy.

Foresight is about understanding macro trends and their implications and producing insight that informs strategic planning. Foresight involves understanding longer-term developments beyond your business or industry, 10 to even 15 years into the future. Understanding these developments and translating them into a business strategy can create unprecedented value, put competitors under pressure, and shape the future of entire industries and markets.

A starting point to develop foresight is compiling reports containing information on demographics, technology, economic development, consumer trends, and interviews with experts and researchers, a mix of qualitative and quantitative data. These more generic reports are typically available for purchase. Industry or segment-specific foresight often needs to be developed by businesses on their own. Organizations can create scenarios by combining and structuring internal and external data and running simulations. These scenarios receive a probability tag and inform a business's long-term strategic trajectory. They become the bigger bets.

For example, let's say you are a sportswear company. Foresight will help you shape your brand and product strategy beyond your current strategic planning cycle. You aim to understand the influence of mega-trends such as urbanization and health. You also investigate technological developments like smartphone usage or blockchain. You throw the population growth and other generic data into the mix and derive scenarios. These aren't necessarily about how the world will develop but are specific to examining relevant fields. The sportswear example includes how people will do and consume sports, virtually and physically. Another field would be sustainability, interpreting what consumers will accept regarding materials or a product's environmental footprint.

Through exploring scenarios and deriving specific information, you identify concrete projects. These projects help you dive deeper into the matter, gather additional insight, and learn as an organization. Projects also serve as reality checks, whether you might be onto something bigger. You define a pilot and aim to accelerate a certain trend that is beneficial for you. As a result, you might consider adjusting your market positioning and the longer-term strategic trajectory of your organization. Up until now, you might have been in the business of selling yoga wear, predominantly to women, in a retail environment. Based on foresight, you decide to pivot from a clothing company to a player in the longevity industry. You help your clients embrace a healthier lifestyle. You supply them with personalized training plans and diets based on extensive AI-backed data analyses. You might even suggest specific medical checkups. The nature of your customer relationship transitions from ad hoc transactions, like money for yoga pants, into long-term partnerships.

Foresight helps you focus and identify the best options to pursue out of myriad possibilities. Through foresight, you silence the ever-nagging fear of missing out. It helps you remove everything you identify as irrelevant, to avoid wasting resources on topics that don't matter. Without using foresight to inform your strategy, you might have decided to grow your business by entering additional geographic markets, adding a yoga line for men, and diversifying your sales channels from retail to mobile sales. There's nothing wrong with that. However, it wouldn't have allowed you to revolutionize your business and tap into the full potential of your customer relationships.

Four Strategic Styles to Choose From

We define what we want to become, personally and professionally. We make decisions that help us become who we want to be. We choose romantic partners that help us grow, study disciplines and hobbies that inspire us, and prioritize how we spend our time and money. Difficult choices and hard decisions are part of the pursuit. Having a goal to work toward helps us through challenging times, and clarity about what we want to achieve empowers us to make the most pivotal choices.

An impact-driven business strategy empowers your organization and your employees. It allows to consciously choose work that helps the organization reach its vision and to drop busy work that you don't profit from, literally or figuratively. The key to a great strategy is having a tangible reason—other than profits—for employees to come to work every day. Make work meaningful and expressive and encourage tangible outcomes. Everyone should understand how they contribute to the bigger picture and why their work matters.

I have witnessed too many overwhelmed businesses and overworked employees. In every case, these situations directly resulted from unaligned expectations and unclear priorities—a lack of strategic clarity. Without strategic clarity, leaders and contributors can't embrace key priorities. Everything seems to be a priority, so it can be hard to rank them. People end up running around like chickens without heads, hustling without focus.

In my previous book, *Secrets of Next Level Entrepreneurs*, I define strategy as a framework that empowers decision making. It describes how we ensure our customers repeatedly choose our offering over a competitor's. In other words, a strategy is a set of key priorities to achieve the desired vision and captures how we create value that will make customers go *wow!* and leave competitors go *huh?*[1]

Before designing a strategy as a framework for decision making, we need to understand the market situation in which a business operates. According to Martin Reeves, a company should consider two critical factors to choose its strategic style: the predictability and the malleability of an industry. Predictability is about how far into the future and accurately you can forecast demand, corporate performance, competitive dynamics, and market expectations. Malleability is the extent to which market players can influence these factors. Reeves defines four types of strategic styles, or archetypes: classical, adaptive, shaping, and visionary.[2]

A *classical* style works best in an industry whose environment is predictable but hard for your company to change. Here, you would target the most favorable market position, analyze, plan, and roll out. These strategies are typically in place for several years. Think oil and gas.

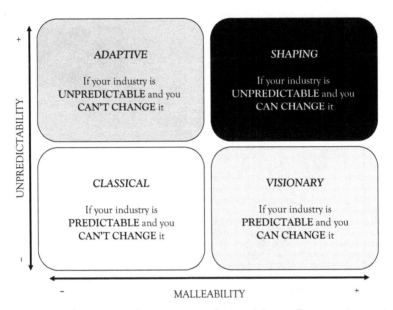

Figure 3.1 Strategy archetypes, according to Martin Reeves

An *adaptive* style is the best style for an uncertain or unpredictable environment, where flexibility trumps long-term planning. You can't predict it; you can't change it. Planning cycles are shorter than in the classical style, and companies would rather move fast and test hypotheses than analyze the last detail before moving. Think of the fashion industry.

The *shaping* style is best suited in an industry with low market entry barriers. Short planning cycles, flexibility, and an experimental approach to strategy are predominant. You can't predict the industry's future, but you can change it. Where an adaptive style focuses on the company itself, a shaping style aims to define entire markets. Think of the Internet.

Finally, a *visionary* style involves knowing the future and creating an entire industry around it, thoroughly planned, and executed, even over a long time. You can predict the changing environment of your industry, and you can shape and mold it. Reeves calls these build-it-and-they-will-come strategies. Think of space tourism.

Strategic planning is medium-term, whereas foresight is about the longer-term future. Both are strategy-related and predict scenarios with varying time horizons and intentions. Signaling is very different: It detects imminent threats to mitigate resulting risks.

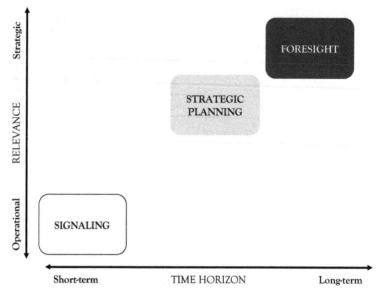

Figure 3.2 Time horizon and relevance of forecasting methods

As an early warning system, signaling informs your response to a crisis that affects business continuity. Some businesses mine data and use algorithms or other technological infrastructure to understand their risk landscape, based on factors they know are disruptive to their operations.

We can look at the U.S. investment bank Morgan Stanley's Fusion Resilience Center, as an example of effective signaling. The firm maintains a program for business continuity management. In early 2020, before the world realized the magnitude of the COVID-19 pandemic, the Fusion Resilience Center signaled a potential threat and triggered corresponding crisis management. When businesses worldwide were scrambling with mandates to work from home, Morgan Stanley's staff hit the ground running. In late March, over 90 percent of the firm was working productively and effectively from home, securing business continuity, and minimizing operational fallout.[3]

Other signaling-based actions include looking for alternative suppliers when armed conflicts and trade wars threaten supply chains. It may also involve adjusting marketing and public relations activities because of public outrage against brands or raising prices early instead of waiting too long when higher-than-usual inflation is looming. Businesses should use signaling, strategic planning, and foresight to thrive short, mid, and long term.

The Role of Culture in Strategy

Historically, a small group of people at the top of an organization made the big decisions, often based on their gut feeling. When data availability and speed of change were still limited, experience- and intuition-based strategy design seemed to work. Today, we drown in data and need to extract relevant information. Volatility, uncertainty, complexity, and ambiguity can exacerbate decision making. The gut feeling doesn't cut it anymore—we need data-backed decisions to secure growth, success, and prosperity.

Foresight is critical to frame questions that address an organization's key challenges over the coming years. Without strategic foresight, you may not even know which questions to ask. Without forward thought, it's impossible to describe the desired future state and equip yourself with the capabilities to deliver.

With foresight, organizations overcome a fixation on looking up to the few on top and relying on their decisions. It opens the strategy process for new ideas, gives more people a voice outside the C-suite, and democratizes strategic decision making. Not every organization is ready for this culture shift that foresight brings along.

In the context of strategy, culture is a crucial aspect. Culture is everywhere. Some call it a secret sauce, not copyable by the competition. Others have a more accidental culture, and trust me, you don't want an accidental culture. I have seen what these cultures do to people. In arbitrarily formed cultures, there are hardly any boundaries, and the doors are open to all kinds of toxic behaviors, like lying, cynicism, gossip, and avoidance of accountability. As a result, people burn out and leave.

Management guru Peter Drucker is often misquoted[4] to have said, "Culture eats strategy for breakfast," pointing out that a company's culture always determines its success, regardless of how effective the strategy may be. Nevertheless, the concept is relevant for strategy processes.

After graduating from business school, I earned my first spurs overseeing the implementation of strategic projects. After we launched an operational excellence (op-ex) program, leadership wanted me to help reshape the organization's sales structures and processes. Inexperienced as I was, I believed that my approach during the op-ex program would also apply to the sales project. I fell flat on my nose and realized that the culture in this department would just let me and all others involved hang out to dry. This behavior was supported and perpetuated by the sales leader of the organization. In other words, leadership didn't have our backs. That's an example of how culture eats strategy, and that's where I agree with the preceding statement about culture eating strategy.

However, I don't agree that culture is the make-or-break factor for strategy. While it is important, people tend to excuse and defend old habits. They attempt to secure their little kingdoms by saying the new strategy goes against the team's culture. It comes off as, "I don't agree with the new strategy, and therefore we will boycott it." To avoid running into these issues on a large scale, it requires empathic leadership and tough decisions to shape culture as part of a strategic initiative, not the other way around. If you align leadership around strategic priorities, culture will not be used as an excuse to dilute strategy.

Consciously created cultures are superchargers for performance and are closely linked to strong strategies. Without a strategic context, what would culture be all about anyway? If we think of culture as the fun and games side of an organization—like table football in the lobby, family events, or free breakfast for everyone—we need to think again. If we understand culture in the light of diversity, equity, inclusion, belonging, and how we shape collaboration, decision making, and communication, then yes, that's certainly part of the picture.

To me, culture is even more than that. It involves how an organization performs, how the job gets done, and how people take individual accountability for results. Culture, as in performance culture. I define performance culture as the result of a psychologically safe workplace where improving performance through learning, experiments, and a quest for the truth is central. As opposed to toxic cultures with a sole emphasis on reaching results by all means. Culture is what people do or don't when no one is watching. Designing and implementing strategy and organizational identity can shape culture as no dedicated culture project can. Let me provide three reasons why this is the case.

The first reason is that so-called culture projects waste time and money. Culture is not an input factor that you can simply fix. Instead, it is a derivative of strategy and leadership. To implement strategy, create impact, and bring values to life, organizations need strong leaders who display a defined set of critical capabilities. Some of the most relevant skills are the abilities to inspire, collaborate, and communicate. This also includes strategic acumen, leading by intention, and selflessness, which we'll explore further in Chapter 7.

The second reason is that executives often shy away from the topic of culture. Either because it is not tangible enough, or because they know it takes time to move the needle, and their incentives are more short term. Or because they simply don't care and believe it to be a topic that HR should address. Instead, if you challenge executives to sharpen the organization's strategy and performance, you'd probably get more eyes and ears on you. If they understand that they can kill two birds with one stone, they will listen. Positioned in such a way, leaders will be more willing to make culture their job.

The third reason is that culture has become a strategic decision factor for investors and other stakeholders. According to Jim Clifton, "If there are two companies with equal shareholder return, but one makes people and the planet sick and the other makes them better, investors will pick the latter."[5] The shift from shareholder to stakeholder capitalism is in full swing, and the responsibility for culture lies with executives. Where they struggle, executives often have boards as sparring partners. Supervisory boards steer the direction of an organization, stress test the strategy, and hire and fire the CEO. Boards are responsible for nudging executive teams toward shaping culture to support the strategic trajectory.

Together with identity, an organization's culture is probably the most important legacy that a leader can build. Identity and culture influence the lives of employees, their families, and friends, long after a leader has moved on. If organizations lead strategy implementation from an impact- and people-centric perspective, they will invariably create a new culture. A culture where everyone focuses on what is important, where they overcome egos, and where they work toward a common goal.

Where leaders act as role models and create opportunities for personal growth. Leaders with such capabilities don't accept behavior and performance detrimental to implementing a strategy or negative for the work environment. Implementing business strategy from this perspective is truly a driving force for culture.

Healthy Habits Are Hard to Establish and Easy to Lose

Repeated behaviors manifest into habits; habits manifest into a culture. They either help or hinder success, personal and professional, individual and organizational. Habits are something mighty. So mighty they can destroy us: drinking, smoking, doing drugs, and eating junk food. Other habits might be less dangerous but harmful nonetheless: excessive social media consumption, binge-watching our favorite streaming site, and not getting enough sleep. And then there are healthy habits—they make us happy: physical exercise, playing an instrument, and spending quality time with our family and friends. Negative habits are often easily adopted and darn difficult to overcome. Harmful habits feed our instant gratification monkey, whereas healthy habits require long-term thinking and sometimes short-term sacrifices. To become proficient at playing an instrument, I might overcome my weaker self here and now and practice rather than relax, if I'd like to reap the benefits later—for example, when enjoying performing with my band at a local music festival. But let's not forget that practice itself is a great source of motivation, seeing the progress we make toward mastery through a habit of exercise and training.

In business, too, there are dangerous, harmful, and healthy habits. A dangerous habit is having too strong a focus on rewards and feeding our egos. If it's all about us, instead of serving clients and the people we lead, the business will go down the drain faster than we might think— examples include the downfall of Lehman Brothers.

Let's talk about three healthy habits for business leaders.

Habit #1: Grow Strategic Acumen

One of the most powerful habits I've seen in business is to grow your ability to think and constantly act strategically. Now, what does that mean? Typically, your everyday business is not strategic but operational. You produce and deliver goods or services, deal with customers, and improve processes and systems to perform effectively and efficiently.

How do you make sure you are able to shift gears from time to time, taking a step back and assessing your business strategically? Everything starts with knowledge. You want to start with building and honing your skills in designing and implementing your business strategy. Strategic acumen helps you avoid the complacency trap and instead establish a habit of strategizing. This will result in you building a better business and more fulfilling life.

Habit #2: Say No by Default

Life is full of sweet temptations and shiny objects: We constantly spot new business opportunities, see the potential for improvements here and there, and want to pursue as many ideas as possible. Imagine your default answer to an idea, opportunity, or offering would always be *yes*, how long would it take before you overburden yourself and those around you?

Strategy is about saying *no* to many potentially great ideas and promising opportunities. You only say *yes* to those that match your strategy in the best possible way and have the biggest potential to propel your business toward the vision you defined. To stay the course, you need to say *yes* to a handful of priorities that receive your time, energy, and money. Everything else gets a *no*. Saying *no* by default will empower you to focus on what matters most.

Habit #3: Check Your Health

It is best practice to check your personal health regularly. New parents take their babies for checkups with a medical doctor at specific intervals. Later in life, we do preventive medical checkups to be sure we are in good shape. Strategically savvy entrepreneurs and leaders do the same for their businesses. At least once a year, they run an organizational health check, focussing on some of the most critical success factors that enable or hinder success.

To determine your company's level of organizational health, set some essential questions to help gauge potential pitfalls. Are we 100 percent certain about the problem that we are uniquely positioned to solve? How does our purpose shine through in our vision, especially concerning our product or service and the value it delivers to customers? Is our business strategy still on point? Does everyone in the organization understand their role in bringing the plan into action and creating the impact we aim for?

Part 1: Executive Summary

The Nine Elements of Organizational Identity

Elements of Identity—Creating High-Performing Organizations

Impact is your purpose translated into action. It provides meaning and credibility.

Principles are underlying values and behavioral guidelines, universally valid.

Mission is what an organization does and for whom. No frills.

Vision is an organization's desired state sometime in the future.

Strategy maps capture strategic priorities to maneuver the organization toward its vision.

Goals are the operational breakdown of strategic KPIs and help move strategy into action.

Targets create motivation and transparency about individual performance.

Capabilities enable leaders and individual contributors to implement identity properly.

Management systems are frameworks to support an organization achieve its strategic and operational objectives.

The Nine Elements of Organizational Identity is a framework and a toolbox for business leaders to grow a legacy in three directions: the people they serve, the organizations they represent, and society as a whole. This Legacy Trident holistically guides their decision making.

Do you have a sweet tooth? Imagine organizational identity as a cake. Impact, principles, and mission are the cake base—on top of the base, vision, strategy, and goals are floating as a thick layer of tasty chocolate buttercream. Targets, capabilities, and management systems make up the top and sides, as its glaze rounds out the look and flavor. I don't know about your preferences; for me, it is usually the creamy, delicious filling in the middle that I love most. But as much as a baker needs the cake base, a strategy needs impact and principles. The three layers of organizational identity include the idealistic base defining an organization, the clear-cut strategy containing the way to success, and the support structures enabling implementation and making it stick.

Why would I suggest that strategy is so central that it sits at the heart of organizational identity? Some might argue that other elements, such as impact and values, or management systems, are equally central. There is a practical reason: imagine how excited your leadership team would be if you asked them to invest money and time into defining impact, values, and behavioral guidelines for your organization. I mean, you can try. If they are impact-driven, intentional individuals, you might have a chance of success with your request.

A strategy process is an ideal vehicle to clarify every aspect of your identity. No other identity element has this power and reach; that is why, strategy is the middle layer touching both base, top, and coating. Strategy is something that leaders typically consider one of their primary responsibilities. It is essential for making investment and hiring decisions for driving the business. So, it typically feels closer to executives than many remaining elements. Talking about impact, values, and behavioral guidelines is far too often seen as some sort of tree-hugger stuff, kind of mushy and intangible, a topic that human resources should deal with, at best. Suppose you address organizational identity in the context of strategy. The chances are your leadership team sees the bigger picture and understands how creating a complete identity aligns the organization for success.

Questions to Explore: Strategy, Purpose, Impact—A Quick Self-Assessment

Check for Strategic Alignment

- To what degree do we have a clear purpose-driven vision and business strategy in place? Are we fully invested in an agreed-upon plan?
- Are we able to link our daily work to this strategy? Do we have an aligned picture of what our strategic priorities are?
- What metrics are we checking regularly to measure positive progress toward our vision?

Test Your Strategy for Purpose

- Which element(s) in our strategy make(s) our hearts glow? Hint: no glow means no purpose.
- How confidently can you identify the magic ingredient in your strategy? Which element(s) go beyond a business rationale, customer satisfaction, innovation, agility, digitalization, or other essential but all too common terms?
- Which element(s) legitimize(s) our organization in the eyes of others, for example, our workforce and communities around us, beyond transactional factors?

Test Your Strategy for Impact

- What is the desired impact of our purpose-infused strategy?
- Are we stopping at purpose and intent or are we creating meaningful action?
- Which tangibility test can we engineer to scrutinize our strategy for impact?

While exploring these questions, you'll probably find answers you are proud of and some you don't like too much. Likely, some answers will seriously challenge you. If the latter is the case, buckle up, get your team together, and create the space you need to develop your strategy and business to the next level.

A Leaders' Guide to Performance Culture

If you want to create culture, approach it from a strategic perspective. It will force you to crystalize your thinking around a set of related topics:

- For the area I lead, what is our contribution to the overarching business strategy?
- How do we measure this contribution, and how often are we talking about these critical metrics?
- To what degree are these metrics translated from an organizational and departmental level to the individual level to make everyone's contribution specific and visible?

- What relevant capabilities do my teams and I need to acquire to succeed and deliver on expectations?
- What is my contribution to helping those around me succeed?
- Am I creating a psychologically safe space for my team to thrive?
- Do I assign work based on people's strengths, interests, passion, and growth opportunities?
- What does celebrating successes—team and individual—look like?
- What behaviors and habits do we support, and which ones do we want to overcome?

The job of a leader is to link the strategic and individual day-to-day levels. As a result, a performance culture emerges where individual contribution matters.

PART 2

Designing Organizational Identity for Peak Performance

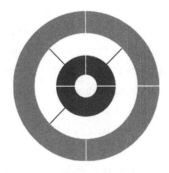

Many people think that strategy is some mysterious process, conducted behind closed doors by people who have special knowledge or, perhaps, special powers. In reality strategy is not a mysterious process. It's not complicated. It's not mystical. It's not difficult to understand. Strategy is simply a plan for gaining an advantage. Nothing mysterious, no special knowledge. But in fact, many people who conduct the strategic process do it very poorly. A few do it really well. And almost everyone can improve on their ability to think strategically.[1]

—Jim Ollhoff, *Strategy 101*

I would go as far as to say everyone can create a winning strategy. We do it constantly in our lives, sometimes in a small and sometimes in a bigger context. If we take Ollhoff's wisdom that strategy is a plan for gaining an advantage, we think and act strategically many times a day. Maybe you strategize as the coach for a neighborhood sports team; you draft a game plan to gain an advantage over the opposing team. Maybe you deliberately plan your executive education to prepare for your next career step and hopefully gain an edge over other candidates. I am sure you have examples in mind of your own daily strategizing.

As a business leader or an established business professional, you have likely participated in strategy or identity processes a few times during your career. Your position, role, and involvement were potentially different each time. The methods might have felt more or less structured and didn't resemble each other. Based on this experience, you might find it challenging to get your head around these processes afresh, time and time again.

This part of the book will be crucial in bringing your identity to life, hands-on. I've broken it down to an eight-step process for designing identity and strategy that you, as a leader or strategist, will put to good use. It contains proven methods and best practices, polished and refined over time. I will suggest ideas on how to structure the process, evaluate where you might want to involve external resources, and share some tips and tricks.

For the most significant part of my career, I have been supporting leaders in for-profit organizations to master business strategy. Sometimes, these strategy projects start on a green field. We sit down to rethink the business and create an entirely new business strategy. In these cases, there are usually only a few predefined factors in place that executive teams need to consider. Sometimes, even larger corporations dare to rethink their business. This approach often applies to flexible companies with relatively low capital expenditure intensity, such as professional services, and new ventures like startups.

Other times, we cannot simply reinvent and therefore derive a new strategy for a certain area of a business from an overarching strategy. Examples include HR strategies that support the overall business strategy, after-sales service strategies that sit within a broader marketing strategy, and business strategies for a specific industry vertical within a larger corporation. No matter the scope of a strategic initiative, the design process described in this section will help you structure the journey.

In Part 2, we'll move into topics such as the mindset leaders should develop as a prerequisite for a successful identity initiative. I'll outline the importance of leadership to bring organizational identity to life. I've also devised and defined three elements in the inner circle of the Nine Elements of Organizational Identity: mission, impact, and principles. And to top that off, I will guide you through a best practice identity and strategy design process, explaining each step.

CHAPTER 4

Strategic Mind-Setting

Collaboration, Commitment, and Consciousness

At a Q&A session of a keynote speech, a participant asked me what matters more for a career: skill or mindset. While we surely need both, I believe mindset is more important than skill when it comes to long-term success. Sure, skill matters, but only so much. Over the long run, people with the right mindset can outperform those who started with better skills.

For example, in sports, when players under the radar suddenly win championships and trophies. Overnight success usually comes from years in the making. In business as well, mindset beats skill. If you have skill but lack perspective, chances are you will not turn your dreams into a reality, let alone build a living legacy. Mindset is more than having belief in oneself, which is a prerequisite. Four distinct mindset shifts paramount for success are the joy of missing out or *JOMO*, speed, abundance, and growth. These four mindsets will help you foster collaboration and commitment to creating a new identity.

FOMO, as we all know, the fear of missing out, drives us into spending our most valuable asset—our attention—on things that don't matter. The antidote to FOMO is JOMO—the joy of missing out. Defining priorities in life and business helps us make the decisions that matter. Knowing where not to spend your time is extremely liberating. It frees us from the urge to follow other people's expectations or strategies. Instead, we create our own paths and success stories.

Speed is a mindset opposite to that of perfectionism. How long does it take to design a perfect strategy? Well, I don't know, because I never did.

We can tweak a strategy forever, seemingly improving it further before saying it's ready. What we are actually doing is standing in the way of implementation, learning, and success. We want to look for *good enough*, not for *perfect*. Keeping an adaptive and open attitude to adjust course while we are implementing will yield more significant results than refining a strategy to the illusion of perfection but failing to deploy it.

Why think in scarcity mode when we can think in abundance? Abundance is about recognizing opportunities and exploring possibilities. It's about curiosity and daring to dream. An abundant mind will bring about new perspectives, thoughts, and discussions that we may never have had before, which is crucial for creating a winning strategy. While JOMO helps us say *no* to a lot of things, an abundance mindset keeps us open-minded so that we don't say *no* prematurely.

Designing a strategy using a growth mindset is superior to that of a fixed mindset. Instead of thinking in absolutes, we think based on a desire to learn. A growth mindset allows us to find new ways of doing things. If we can internalize growth, we'll be able to take different paths, and learn additional skills. We ask the right questions, such as "What am I missing?" or "How could I use this negative experience and turn it into something positive?"

Organizational psychologist Adam Grant describes two concepts that help bring these four mindsets to life: challenge networks and confident humility. A challenge network is a team around us that consists of people who can disagree agreeably, giving brutally honest feedback without being personal or aggressive. The purpose of a challenge network is to question assumptions, overcome blind spots, and counterbalance potential weaknesses in our thinking. Go for speed in execution and learning, and use your challenge network to adjust direction.

Confident humility is "having faith in our capability while appreciating that we may not have the right solution or even be addressing the right problem. That gives us enough doubt to re-examine our old knowledge and enough confidence to pursue new insights."[1] The sweet spot of confidence is when we believe in ourselves and simultaneously doubt that we have all the right tools in place.

Adopting these mindsets throughout a business requires consciousness and commitment. Think about your leadership team for a moment: how trustful is the collaboration among the team members? Are team meetings draining, or are you leaving them energized? Are they a waste of time, or do they motivate you? Is the collaboration characterized by mutual trust, or are discussions more about who is right or wrong, or fighting about resources? Do you hold healthy, productive conflict in your challenge network, or are you stubbornly blind to rethinking your ways? Are you caught up in relationship conflicts, or focused on solving a task?

Quarreling leadership teams can hardly design a powerful strategy, let alone an organizational identity. Dysfunctional leadership teams usually consist of unconscious leaders, at least partly. Conscious leaders don't engage in negative conflict, stay silent when they should speak up, or avoid accountability.

Conscious leadership is an enabler of organizational identity. Without consciousness, leadership teams cannot dig deep enough, and strategy initiatives will invariably fail to deliver the expected results. If we don't search deep enough, the resulting organizational identity can easily be debunked as a superficial construct.

Imagine consciousness as a state of mind that puts us either above or below an imaginary line. Above the line, we appear open, curious, and committed to learning. It is where we ask questions unarguably and listen deeply. As a result, we foster creativity, innovation, connection, and collaboration. Below the line, we are defensive, closed, and want to be right.[2]

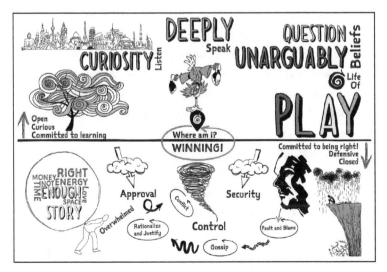

Figure 4.1 Locating yourself, by Conscious Leadership Group and Graeme Franks

There is no way we can create strategy and identity below the line. By contrast, functional leadership teams—invariably consisting of more conscious leaders—take organizational identity by storm. Therefore, before you even think about engaging a team in a strategy or identity process, assess how functional the team is and how conscious everyone is.

We often misjudge how dysfunctional teams really are. Far too often, I have nudged executives to address dysfunctional behavior among their team members early in the process, just to see them ignore the issue. Their reactions ranged from "I can't see any issue" to "Everything will be fine in the end." Trust me, it won't—especially not if the unconscious mind of the leader is the issue.

Combining Strategy and Team Development Yields Greater Results

Instead of creating a functional team first, leaders would jump right into the action, trying to achieve results without investing in those who deliver them. The good news is that a strategy process is an excellent vehicle for creating an organizational identity and the perfect vehicle to build a functional team. Weaving team development efforts into a strategy process will help the team practice vulnerability and engage in positive conflict immediately.

Tackling team strategy and identity development in an integrated way might take a little longer than just focusing on strategy. It's worth the extra effort as it results in deeper conversations, more productive conflict, and higher levels of commitment and accountability. Creating psychological safety and becoming a functional team allow the team to aim high rather than playing it safe. Your strategy will be more ambitious, and the team will be able to accelerate the execution process. Removing barriers eliminates the blindside of hiding them in the design process and letting them resurface later.

To achieve that, leaders need to become humble learners. *Humble* means exploring options, curiously, without thinking: *been there, seen that, got it on a t-shirt.* No one can design a great strategy on their own, no one is better off alone than with the team. Humble yourself by learning about your peers, their hopes, dreams, aspirations, fears, thoughts, and feelings. Acknowledge them.

Figure 4.2 Team development and strategy design embedded in identity design

The *learner* stands for the style of leadership. Instead of a directive, transactional leadership style, apply a transformational coaching style. Learners don't broadcast an opinion, hoping to convince others. Fixed beliefs don't support discussions. Defending our turf doesn't help the team. What helps teams thrive are curious, challenging, and exploratory questions that foster positive conflict in search of the best way forward. And the best ideas don't correlate with title or rank; therefore, listen, be a curious explorer of ideas, and pay attention. If you can become a humble learner, it will result in deeper conversations and connections.

When Hollywood Star Joseph Gordon-Levitt spoke about the topic of attention during the 2019 TED conference, he emphasized the importance of paying attention over getting attention. Instead of craving attention, practice paying attention to what others feel, to what those around you dream of. Gordon-Levitt describes the magic of paying attention as the key to creativity.[3]

Detach Yourself From Ego-Driven Aspirations

In the context of strategy and identity design, leaders need to detach themselves from ego-driven aspirations and behavior, instead curiously immersing themselves into the design process. A new strategy will bring change for the organization and you as a leader. Examples include changes in leadership responsibility and scope of work, different ways of working, and learning new capabilities. You would rather shape this future than be shaped by it. You cannot shape the future when everyone on the team is clinging to past achievements or things, they feel belong to them.

I cannot overstate the importance of talking freely and designing identity-based options rather than manipulating your future around current responsibilities. Free yourself from the present and past. Some current positions might not be necessary to fulfill in the future; don't design around people and titles. The organizational setup follows strategy, and if you can develop a plan for the future, there will always be a place for you, in this or another organization. With that in mind, the all-dominant success factor for your search for strategy and identity can blossom through collaboration.

Remember the dark ages, when a strategy was kept secret, written as a mysterious document, presumably kept in the locked desk drawer of the patriarchal leader of an organization? Fortunately, those times are over. Today's world has become so complex and fast-paced that only a collaborative approach to strategy, leadership, and identity will yield desirable results. Collaboration is the lubricant that keeps your organization running smoothly to achieve performance levels and outcomes never seen before. It is a key ingredient in building high-performance teams and organizations.

If you don't buy into shaping a functional leadership team as the key to success, I suggest we take a look at former Finnish mobile phone giant

Nokia. The downfall of what used to be one of the most valuable brands is attributed to various unfortunate decisions by Nokia's leadership. Within a few years, between 2007 and 2013, Nokia ruined its mobile phone business. From a market share of about 40 percent, they went to sell off their swaying mobile phone division. The brand nearly fell into oblivion. At the core of these decisions, researchers saw a dysfunctional leadership body suffering from deep internal rivalries.[4] This example should serve as a warning for those feeling consciousness and psychological safety are only for tree-huggers.

With the mindset of a humble learner, we can let go of the urge to pretend we know it all. Be honest about it. Publicly state that you don't know how the result of your identity process will look. If you pretend to know it all, people will become sceptical about you as a leader and even lose faith in you. Instead, reduce airtime, and listen, become a facilitator rather than an opinion leader.

When We Talk, We Cannot Listen

When I consulted a municipality in Ontario, Canada, on drafting a new economic development plan, we involved a private sector committee. After selecting the committee members, we facilitated a workshop with the representatives, in which we collected and structured their views on economic development.

To our initial surprise, the Mayor decided not to attend the workshop. He left the stage to those he wanted to listen to and trusted us to steer the process. By taking himself out of the equation, the Mayor avoided potentially influencing or even dominating the discussions. No one felt the need to prequalify ideas for agreement. In the culmination of the workshop, the committee then presented a fresh proposal to the Mayor.

We learn by listening and asking questions. To force us to shut up, we can either follow the Mayor's example and exclude ourselves to allow room for external input or assign ourselves the role of a facilitator, rather than participating. Facilitators ask questions to help a group succeed, and it might be hard to maintain this role throughout the entire process. After all, you have valuable contributions to make. Find help and involve a strategy facilitator that can propel the team's quest to overcome dysfunctions while also managing everyone's airtime. A strategy facilitator holds you in the process, leads you through each step, and helps you to avoid mistakes.

Advantages of internal and external facilitators for identity processes	
Internal	External
• Know the organization: processes, policies, understand internal lingo	• Bring experience, expert knowledge, and fresh perspectives from outside the organization, ideally across industries; they know the process end-to-end
• At least initially, might be more trusted than an *outsider*, as they belong to the organization	
• Know history, past efforts, and context of the current situation; they might have been involved in comparable initiatives in the past	• Are unbiased in their approach and create a neutral atmosphere, to help reach the best possible outcome
	• Ask the difficult questions and confront assumptions, challenge internal paradigms and people regardless of their position
• Know participants and stakeholders, and their opinions; might have working relationships with them (which can cause biases)	
• Often easier on the budget	• Are not personally affected by decisions and can therefore move the group forward when dealing with difficult or controversial issues

CHAPTER 5

Rolling Up the Sleeves

Mission, Impact, and Principles

You might have realized that I sometimes use the term *strategy design* synonymously with *identity design*. It underlines the importance of a strategy process as a vehicle for defining all elements of organizational identity. However, strategy and identity are not the same. Strategy is an integral part of organizational identity; neither can sustainably exist without the other. The following process will help you design organizational identity using a strategy process at its core.

Let me preface this chapter by saying that this eight-step process might feel too extensive or laborious for the organization you lead. Adjust the process to your needs by applying what makes sense for the type and size of your business or department. I invite you to explore each step to discover which parts feel essential and applicable to your specific situation.

Figure 5.1 displays the eight steps of identity design. While it is a process—a sequence of steps to go through in a particular order—I deliberately leave out arrows in these figures. Instead of a linear process, it is more about connectedness: The figures display a set of essential components, each one contributing to the whole. More often than not, identity design requires us to go back and forth rather than following a straight line. Now, let me walk you through these steps, to help explore what works best for you.

Note: On my website, I provide a field guide for your strategy and identity initiative. It contains templates, exercises, manuals, charters, lists, and questionnaires that give you the head start you need. Visit https://brueckmann.ca/fieldguide for access.

Figure 5.1 *Building blocks of the identity design process*

Step 1: Executive Interviews

Outcome

- Topics of strategy and identity are accessible
- Level of strategic acumen among the team assessed

Participants: All members of the leadership team

Length: 30 to 45 minutes, per interviewee

Standard: At a minimum, all opinion leaders interviewed (if not the entire leadership team)

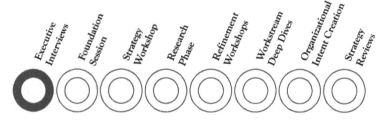

Figure 5.2 *Executive interviews at the start of the identity design*

Before starting the process, it's ideal that you explore the terrain you are building the initiative on, especially if you recently joined the organization and are now leading the initiative. You want to dip your toe into the water and check the temperature, instead of jumping in head-first. Make sure you understand the willingness and excitement of the team toward designing a new strategy. Learn about individual experiences from earlier projects and fathom the level of strategic understanding. It's essential to collect insights and inform your approach. Then you can open the strategy discussion before gathering the core team for the first workshop. This is particularly helpful if the strategy hasn't been a top priority recently, or if previous strategies might have drifted into limbo. The stimulus you produce will help your team push-start their strategy brains.

A straightforward way to achieve this insight is to run executive interviews. The interviews shouldn't resemble an inquisition but rather be an open discussion about the interviewee's thoughts regarding strategy. Depending on the level of trust within the team, involving a third party—internal or external—to run the interviews and consolidate the result might be a good idea. With a third party intervening, you create a safe, confidential environment where people are more likely to speak freely and share their thoughts more openly.

Sample Questions

- What are the key objectives that the organization needs to achieve in the coming years?
- How well is the leadership population aligned with these objectives?
- To what degree will these objectives challenge the organization?

Answering these questions requires a certain level of reflection, strategic acumen, and the ability to recognize and admit mistakes. The more overt and unguarded responses to these questions will lead to a solid position to approach the foundation session to follow. Once the interviews are complete, the results should be consolidated into a report and presented back when the team meets for the first time.

Step 2: Foundation Session

Outcome

- Understanding of unique strengths of the organization
- Alignment on foreseeable challenges and commitment to the process ahead
- Clarity on mission, purpose, desired impact, and principles

Participants: The core team for the design phase, consisting of (parts of) the leadership team of an organization, division, or department; potentially additional experts

Length: 1.5 to 2 days

Standard: Before moving to the next stage (the strategy workshop), make sure you have achieved at least 80 percent results for each preceding outcome listed.

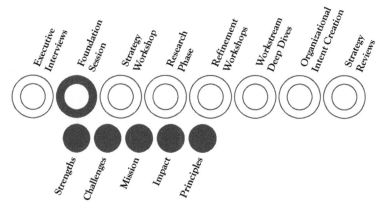

Figure 5.3 Content and flow of a foundation session

A friend once told me how much he enjoys riding the ancient tractor they use on his family's farm, "There are so many moving parts all running flat out all the time and you must be really careful shifting it up a gear so everything lines up perfectly. But once it's in gear you're off to the races!" That's how a company might feel—a bit rusty, powerful but slightly dated in how it functions, and you can't just force it into a higher gear. Before a strategy workshop, there are a few moving parts you want to align carefully. Therefore, instead of risking a breakdown when shifting gears, make sure the pieces are in place and ready for what's coming their way.

The foundation session serves two major purposes. The first is a diagnosis to determine which elements of identity are in place and to what degree. Keeping in mind our cake analogy from Part 1, we can measure the base layer, gauging if it consists of purpose, impact, and principles. At this stage, the leadership team is assessed for clarity on what the organization does and for whom, asserting that the mission is crisp and clear. I often find there is at least some direction available for the team, even if some elements would be undefined.

It's not often that a corporation will redefine its values and behavioral guidelines, let alone its desired impact. Even if an organization regularly reviews its elements of organizational identity—what they should certainly do—they will likely develop its identity further, rather than starting from scratch time and time again. However, it may be the case that your organization is unclear of its foundational identity elements. If so, I suggest taking a detour. Instead of starting with strategy design right away, start by creating the base layer of the cake first.

If you lead somewhere in the middle of your organization, you should not wait for someone to close these gaps. There might be an element of identity missing for the organization—don't let that stop you from taking the lead and shaping the future for your area of responsibility. Let's assume your organization has a solid base layer in place: impact, values, and behavioral guidelines are defined. Review these elements and use the opportunity to translate them into action.

The second goal of foundation sessions is to align the team around the need for a new strategy process. There might still be some resistance as to whether a new strategy is needed. Even if there is a consensus, some might feel now is not the right time to start. A new strategy should be seen as equally important and urgent among the leadership team to embark on such a journey. You need their buy-in and commitment for the process ahead. Whether you achieve your peers' commitment strongly connects to the perceived importance and urgency of designing a new strategy.

It has been a long time since I met a leader who denied the need for a clear-cut strategy. The importance of having one in place seems to be widely accepted and rarely challenged. Regarding the level of urgency, however, you might find a more diverse picture and differing opinions among the team. A low level of motivation might originate from one of two positions. It may be that the business is running well, and we are so swamped right now, and it's not a good time for a new strategy. Or it could be that the business is in poor shape, we must take care of our customers, or there won't be a company left to implement a new strategy.

The most common reason for pushback, which I hear all too often, is that everything is going great and there is no need for a new strategy. At the heart of this statement lies excitement about how well the business is operating. It might look like a brilliant idea to focus entirely on reeling in the herring as long as it is close to the coast. Take what you can get now, it might be gone tomorrow.

There is nothing wrong with enjoying success. It is, however, dangerous to become complacent during times of success. In the mid- and long term, this attitude can make any organization miss the right moment to rethink their business for future success. When the herring is gone, it can be difficult to pivot. When massive change occurs, these moments are strategic inflection points, and a company must adapt extremely fast or fail.

Great leaders prepare their organization for such moments by having a strategy that can be adjusted, rather than starting with a strategy process from scratch. At strategic inflection, organizations don't have enough time to start at the beginning. Admittedly, leaders can appear slightly paranoid when initiating the design of a new strategy while everyone else seems to enjoy the good times. Intel cofounder Andy Grove's take on such moments is that *Only the Paranoid Survive*, and so titled his book about the opportunities of strategic inflection points.[1]

Famous companies that were not paranoid enough include the Canadian technology firm formerly known as Research in Motion, now Black-Berry Limited, and the American photography company Kodak. These companies enjoyed years, if not decades, of success and became too complacent to reinvent themselves through new strategies. As a result, the companies and their brands lost market share and value until they became insignificant or disappeared completely.

Another reason a company may not consider implementing a new strategy is when the business is running poorly. There is an implied panic mode where it becomes a rush to take care of revenues primarily, letting strategy fall to the wayside. The driving factor is fear of losing customers, sales, income, and jobs. Leaders should recognize these fears and take them seriously—address them and manage them. Instead of allowing negative self-fulfilling prophecies and excuses for avoiding a strategy process, facilitate a discussion based on facts and create transparency. If the result of a fact-based conversation is that the company is far from being a case for restructuring, the excuse won't stand the test. Remove angst from the team before you embark on your strategy journey.

If the organization was close to bankruptcy, the level of urgency among leaders will be as high as it can get. But if the platform is on fire, restructuring the company should be the order of the day. Restructuring is not a strategy as such. In Part 1, I discussed four strategic archetypes a business can choose, depending on the malleability and predictability of its industry. Martin Reeves originally defined five archetypes, the latter-most being *renewal*. It comes into play when operating in a harsh business environment. He argues that this initially defensive approach should be applied when resources are severely constrained. After an initial phase of economizing by refocusing the business, a company must move toward one of the other four archetypes to secure its future. In other words, strategy design starts once a company is back in calmer waters.

When starting a foundation session, check in with the team to understand the necessity and sense of urgency regarding a strategy process. Let's assume on a scale from 1 to 10, with 10 being the highest, the feedback sits below an 8 for either or both importance and urgency. Such low values are not ideal because a strategy process in the context of organizational identity is a team marathon that you want to run together. It requires lasting energy, time, and money. If your team sees little importance or urgency, starting the process could mean you embark on a suicide mission. Parts of the team will likely chicken out once the process becomes difficult. They will lack commitment and engagement and will not develop the amount of accountability needed to create an impact-driven and winning strategy. This would leave you, as a leader, isolated.

At the beginning of this section, I defined the standard that you should aim for in the foundation session as 80 percent. This is a different way of saying, aim for results that are good enough, not perfect. I've seen teams go down rabbit holes and waste hours on unimportant details, in the grand scheme of things. Avoid the perfection myth and realize that this is just the beginning of a longer process. Don't let emotionally charged discussions distract you from what matters. Focus on the 80 percent that will let you move ahead, instead of trying to complete the final 20 percent toward perfection. Done is sometimes better than perfect.

Aligning on the Unique Strengths of an Organization

If the average on perceived urgency and importance are low at the start of the foundation session, this part of the session becomes even more important. Aligning the team around the strengths is a positive and reasonably easy start. It feels good to talk about strengths as often the atmosphere among the group will lighten up during the conversation. People may even crack jokes. You want to create an accessible atmosphere—encouraging each individual to participate and get the ball rolling. Ease the team into the discussion, while potentially preparing them for the more difficult topics to come.

You will quickly collect a solid list of strengths that the team attributes to the organization. At times, the discussion might even feel a bit all over the place, with participants throwing in strengths of different kinds, such as strengths of a certain department or team, strengths around certain structures and processes, and sometimes strengths that others on the team don't even see. Let it flow! You may want to capture what you hear on a flip chart to help the group discuss each strength freely.

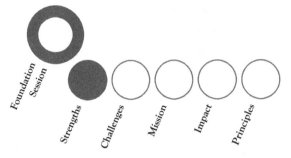

Figure 5.4 Content of a foundation session—strengths

Once the team has discussed their thoughts, challenge them to iden-tify those strengths on the list, which they can claim as unique to their business. In other words, which of these strong points cannot be claimed by a competitor, to the best of your knowledge?

The outcome will help you later in the design process, for example, it serves as a starting point in your analysis of the strengths, weaknesses, opportunities, and threats (SWOT) to your business. Understanding your strengths also links to how you create value for your customers, a core element of any successful business strategy. Finally, knowing your strengths will help you master the expected challenges ahead.

Challenges, Implications, and the Necessary Capabilities to Tackle It All

Rather than immediately starting a discussion about future challenges, first help your team reach a common understanding of the past.

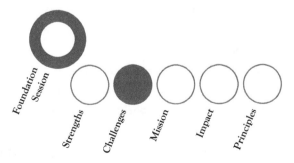

Figure 5.5 Content of a foundation session—challenges

Maybe the organization has overcome major challenges. Maybe some members have joined the team only recently and are not aware of important stepping stones used over the past years. Before you talk about the future, align on the path you took to get here. This is the moment to be conscious about your recent history—successes and downfalls. It's a great time to give yourselves a pat on the shoulder for the bigger achievements.

Additionally, aligning on the past will reveal if the organization has been carrying around unaddressed issues. For some individuals, it's a necessary step to help them mentally detach from operational topics in the present, taking a different perspective to reflect, and to start thinking more strategically. Make sure you help the team address internal and external challenges one at a time. Strategy work is all about creating clarity. By separating internal and external factors, you clear up assumptions and separate facts from opinions.

From here, we enter uncharted territory. The team engages in a discussion about the future, and the challenges they expect coming their way. Inevitably, the years ahead are uncertain, and the discussion shifts from a fact-based conversation about the past toward an assumption-based discussion about the future.

The dynamics may change as there will be people in the room with ideas and beliefs about the coming years. Your role as a leader or facilitator is to bring balance to the discussion and make sure everyone contributes their viewpoints. It's essential that all opinions be heard to achieve clarity about what the organization is headed for. Remember, you want to achieve buy-in and commitment among the team; the goal is 8 or higher on importance and urgency.

Once the team accepts the challenges ahead, help them explore what these mean for them, pertaining to all leaders in the organization. This is the group of people that will have to guide the organization through the picture you just painted. And this picture is most likely more concrete than the list of challenges every individual initially had in their own heads. As a result, it might feel overwhelming seeing all these challenges written down in front of them.

Help the team explore these feelings and resulting implications, to make them tangible. The team might mention certain competencies that are needed to face the challenges. Capture these thoughts as you will revisit the list later in the process when you think about equipping leaders with relevant capabilities to lead the process of implementing organizational identity.

Clarify Organizational Mission, Impact, and Principles

I have yet to meet an organization that has all elements of identity clearly defined, let alone ingrained in their daily business. And if this is the case in your area of responsibility, too, it is your chance to leave a mark by getting your hands on those elements and starting to shape the future.

Mission—What We Do and for Whom (and What We Don't Do)

Once the team is aligned on the urgency of a strategy process, review your organizational mission, impact, and principles. The easiest to tackle should be your mission statement, a description of what you do and for whom.

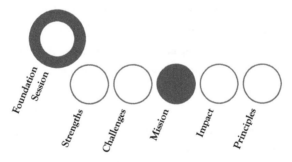

Figure 5.6 Content of a foundation session—mission

Assume you are the CEO of a luxury hotel chain, owning vacation resorts and business hotels across Asia and the Middle East. A potential mission could be: We rent out short-term accommodation and provide recreational and business facilities and services to individuals and organizations. No fancy adjectives, no marketing verbiage. Plain and simple, providing clarity, leaving minimal room for interpretation. Valid for years to come.

Your mission implies the industry you are in, the competition you deal with, the regulatory environment; these are key aspects of your market and competitive analysis later in the process. Your mission must be strongly linked to the timeframe of your strategy. It usually doesn't take core teams much time to define their organization's business. However, I remember a client having a wild discussion about their mission. They split into groups and drafted different statements, which partly overlapped, and then tried to combine them into one. The result was a monstrosity containing various buzzwords. I read the result out loud to the team—and they started laughing, realizing how far off they were from what they intended to create. An hour later, the team had formulated a mission statement that was still baseline generic but had an interesting twist: "As partners to our stakeholders we deliver support directly and through leadership to our teams, today and tomorrow." The magic of this statement revealed itself at second glance only. First, if we strip it down to the absolute core, the mission statement would read like this: We deliver support to our stakeholder. This leadership team oversaw the after-sales service operations of a larger organization. Delivering technical support was exactly what they did. And because they did so for many different groups, internal and external, they called their audience stakeholders, rather than customers or clients. Instead of stripping away all nonessential aspects, they used the mission statement to stress aspects that felt important to them and hadn't found their way into any other element of their organizational identity.

First, they reminded themselves that they should not be pushed around and instead stand their ground, as they knew best what great support looks like. That's why they included "as partners," as in "at eye-level." Second, the appendix "today and tomorrow" was a great way of pointing out that the leadership team was in it for the longer run, and not first and foremost to advance their individual careers, moving on when the next opportunity arose. And third, the interesting twist I mentioned was that they added "directly and through leadership to our teams." Based on how we defined mission earlier in the book, they not only captured their business, but also their contribution and value as a leadership team. Thereby, the statement became a mission statement and a commitment to their teams and to each other at the same time.

Impact—The Reason of Your Existence as an Organization

While defining your business and capturing it as a mission statement should be a quick win, the next step will typically result in longer and more in-depth discussions. Answering the question why your organization exists might not always be easy. Don't be distracted by a shareholder value-type answer. Return on capital invested, paying out salaries, or providing job security are purely transactional factors and don't qualify as a higher purpose.

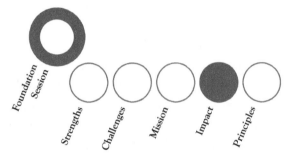

Figure 5.7 *Content of a foundation session—impact*

The north star of your organization needs to go beyond anything transactional. Your organization should aim to fulfill a transformational purpose. Fellow strategist Graham Kenny shared advice to bear in mind, "Inspire your staff to do good work for you, find a way to express the organization's impact on the lives of customers, students, patients—whomever you're trying to serve. Make them feel it."[2]

In fact, don't write a generic purpose statement. Go beyond purpose and craft a specific impact statement, capturing what your organization will bring to the lives of employees, society, the environment, and our planet. Impact is what gives you legitimacy. It should be taken seriously, as it defines what you are or what you want to become as an organization. In addition, it should be measurable, at least to a certain degree. It's one thing to formulate a grand statement, and another thing to hold yourself accountable to that aspiration. Give it the necessary grounding. Make it specific and measurable to give it more space to swim, not sink.

A great impact statement is far from being shallow; the more specific, the better your chance to measure how well you are following that call.

In Part 1, we discussed three examples—let's see if they hold up and are measurable.

- Environment protection organizations, private and public: *to protect wildlife and preserve natural resources and habitat*
- Food banks and hunger-relief charities: *to collect and distribute food helping people struggling with hunger*
- UNHCR—The United Nations High Commissioner for Refugees agency: *to safeguard the rights and well-being of refugees*

Environmental protection agencies typically target geographic areas, such as nearshore waters, or they support endangered species, or address human causes of the destruction of habitat or climate. Food banks and hunger-relief organizations operate mainly locally, supporting those in need in certain neighborhoods, schools, and shelters. The UNHCR reacts to emergencies, for example, helping Rohingya refugees in Bangladesh, fleeing genocide in Myanmar, or the many emergencies in Africa and the Middle East. In addition, the organization addresses a wide variety of topics from raising education levels, providing access to health care, and fighting sexual exploitation.

These statements are clearly measurable indeed, with initiatives being directly derived from their purpose to create specific impact. As the success of these initiatives is measurable, the statement as such is quantifiable in numbers: lives saved, meals handed out, children vaccinated, tents built, animals rescued, poaching cases reduced, area of habitat preserved, and measures or laws put in place by governments, advocated for by these organizations.

Years ago, I consulted with a business whose purpose statement proclaimed that they wanted to raise the quality of life of their customers; at the same time, the company tricked customers into buying their products. Not every organization can credibly claim to have a higher purpose, even if they might have a polished statement in place. If you examine these statements and benchmark them against their actions, you can distinguish between fake and real purposes.

If your organization doesn't have a defined impact statement—it is time you start digging. Chances are you will uncover the purpose and desired impact of your organization by discussing it with your team. If you struggle to identify this fundamental part of your business, you have two options: either re-evaluate your professional trajectory and join an organization whose impact resonates with you. Or you reshape your current organization and identify its true purpose and desired impact.

Principles—Values and Resulting Behavioral Guidelines

Organizational values are an interesting topic that is fun to explore. Let's take a pen and paper and write down the first 10 positively attributed organizational values you can think of. You likely populate your list with such words as honesty, fairness, and excellence. And therein lies the issue.

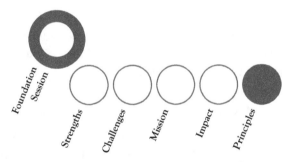

Figure 5.8 Content of a foundation session—principles

According to British ethics professor and corporate philosopher Roger Steare, there are 10 so-called moral values[3]:

Wisdom	I think through my decisions carefully
Fairness	I treat others fairly and with respect
Courage	I stand up for my beliefs and do what's right
Self-control	I am patient and self-disciplined
Trust	I am trustworthy, reliable, and also trusting to others
Hope	I encourage others to be positive
Humility	I am less important than the team
Love	I am empathetic and care about other people
Honesty	I speak the truth and encourage others to be open
Excellence	I try to do my best in everything I do

I'd argue that every decent human being and upright organization should strive to achieve these 10 moral values. Consequently, the list helps us understand that corporate values need more than just fundamental moral values. Moral values are must-have values. Without these in place, an organization cannot live up to a higher purpose, let alone make an impact.

I am not suggesting these cannot be values for an organization; on the contrary, these values must underpin everything you do; thus, *must have*. There is nothing wrong with including a must-have value in your organizational values to substantiate the importance. But if any other organization could claim your values as their own, they are not unique to you, and it is time you rework your set of values.

In the foundation session, collect your must-have values and briefly describe their significance. You will revisit them later and incorporate them into behavioral guidelines, to help your people understand what they mean in action. Now, discover the set of values that is unique to you, and potentially no other organization can claim. They should be non-negotiable and enduring.

I recommend building on the impact statement you drafted earlier in the session. Ask yourself which values are clearly linked to and fully support your impact. Ideally, they are at the heart of your organization already. There might be two or three; I call these diamond values: unique, enduring, hard to alter, even under pressure. Just like a diamond. You may identify values that are not strongly visible today but should be manifested soon. Even if they are leaning more toward an ambition than a reality today, include them in your set of values, marking them as an ambition value. Then, define a crystal-clear path on how you want to engrain them into your culture.

Explore values from the perspective of companionate love, as in feelings of affection, caring, compassion, and tenderness. Professor Sigal Barsade of the Wharton School of the University of Pennsylvania studied the effects of value-based cultures and companionate love. She found evidence of better employee engagement, more teamwork, less burnout, less absenteeism, and better customer satisfaction. In cultures based on companionate love, where people care about one another, employees feel a higher commitment to the organization and show more personal accountability because they want to, not because they must. This type of culture is what Barsade called emotional culture, defining what emotions people should express, promote, and talk about, whereas a cognitive culture defines how people should behave based on rationality, for example, being result-oriented or law-abiding.[4]

If you let companionate love inform your search for values, the outcome will help your employees and your bottom line. The question is whether you, as a leader, are ready to be a role model for these values and bring them to life within your organization.

Once you have your values defined, create a rationale around them, to help your people understand them in the way you intend. Investment bank and financial services firm Morgan Stanley describes their core values as part of its code of conduct. One of Morgan Stanley's core values is "Doing the Right Thing":

> We (...) make ethical and informed decisions and take personal responsibility for our actions. (...) Asking yourself questions about an action can help you decide how to proceed.
> - Does my action comply with (...) applicable laws, regulations and our policies?
> - Is my action consistent with this Code and our core values?
> (...)
> If you are unsure (...), seek guidance from your supervisor (...) or your HR representative.[5]

Explaining values provides context and helps employees understand and embrace them. Laying down the expectations is a prerequisite for translating values into observable behaviors to form both an emotional and cognitive culture.

Additional Content for a Foundation Session and Following Steps

A foundation session should include a discussion about what strategy is, to align on terminology and understanding. In addition, the team should dive into the results from the executive interviews you ran before the session. The results report will contain insights that help the team avoid repeating past mistakes.

Before closing the foundation session, agree on the way forward—the next step could be a strategy design workshop. Agree on a date and consider who to include as contributors. These contributors should possess strategic acumen, detach themselves from their current role and position, and bring skills that the leadership team may be lacking. Pick the participants wisely, bearing in mind that these people might take over responsibilities, for example, lead a workstream, or become part of the strategy core team.

It may be wise to consider administrative support for your identity process and staff your project management office (PMO). These bring structure to the process and will support necessary leg work. Be intentional about whom you want to have on board. Ask yourself whether candidates bring the right mindset and skillset for what you are about to embark on, strategy design.

CHAPTER 6

The Chocolate Buttercream

Identity's Strategic Centerpiece

Now that we have a foundation drafted, it's time to shift gears into a commercial context. In Step 3, we discuss how to design the core of your organizational identity. Do you remember the cake analogy we previously introduced? Have your fork ready. Here comes the chocolate buttercream.

Step 3: Strategy Design Workshop

Outcome

- Draft of vision statement written
- Strategic KPI dashboard created
- Workstreams outlined and strategy map drafted

Participants: Strategy core team, at this stage, likely the entire leadership team, plus selected additional contributors

Length: two full days, in-person.

Standard: Before moving on to the next stage (research phase), ensure you reach an agreement on which workstreams you would like to detail further if you need to prioritize.

The strategy workshop involves creating three tangible outcomes: vision, with key performance indicators or KPIs, and workstreams, all captured in a draft version of a strategy map. The vision outlines the desired future of your organization. You derive a set of strategic KPIs to measure progress toward the vision. And workstreams drive these KPIs in the right direction.

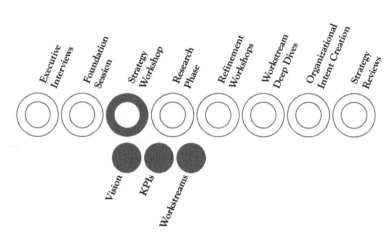

Figure 6.1 Content and flow of a strategy workshop

At the beginning of this workshop, challenge the participants to apply a creative mindset. Help them stretch their thinking beyond what seems possible or realistic. At this early stage, doubt and negative thinking can be detrimental to forward motion. Green light thinking is what you need, rather than operating within limiting beliefs.

If you limit your creativity, you likely step into a trap many strategy projects ended in: Instead of a winning strategy, you might create a business continuity plan or an operational excellence program. This would send a message to the organization, demonstrating the lack of vision for the future.

No organization is immune to falling into this trap. An example is the fast-food giant McDonald's. Their strategy is built on three key pillars: They aim to retain customers, regain customers they have previously lost, and convert their casual customers into regular customers.[1] In my opinion, and with added irony, McDonald's strategy is a bit thin: sell more products to more customers, more often. Who would have thought a company might want to grow its customer base and increase buying frequency? Remember the strategy self-assessment in the Summary of Part 1: How confidently can you identify the magic ingredient in your strategy? If you can locate a magic ingredient in the preceding example, please help me find it.

Key Outcome #1: New Vision Statement

Once your creative mindset is driving, it's time to cruise on. The first tangible outcome you want to create in the strategy design workshop is your organization's new vision. I've seen a wide variety of vision statements, some shorter, some longer. Some statements listed quantified goals, others didn't; some were inspiring but vague. Some listed specific target markets and innovation goals, while others didn't even have a defined timeframe. I concluded that a vision can best be described as an organization's desired state sometime in the future, an aspirational statement that articulates what an organization would like to become and achieve, providing orientation and inspiring action.

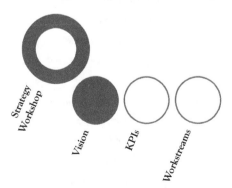

Figure 6.2 Content of a strategy workshop—vision

But where do you start? Teams usually brainstorm and gather a list of ideas reflecting individual wishes and aspirations, often fluffy and bold. They touch on desires like becoming innovation champions, delivering best-in-class service, or revolutionizing how customers engage with the business. I've also seen statements about creating a global footprint, building an integrated IT landscape, and investment in research and development. Sometimes, the core team would discuss customer value, throw in revenue targets or capital market metrics, and even mention specific target clients.

Let it flow. At this stage, ideas are often just the first ideas, not necessarily best ideas. Some of them might find their way into the vision eventually, depending on where your core team sits in an organization. If you are the leader of a sales department, the vision your core team would design will (hopefully) differ from the vision of a procurement department within the same company. And both visions will hopefully align with the overall company vision.

The odds are that not many individuals in the core team have solid experience in drafting a vision. A pitfall I often observe is that businesses look for a quick win, a bold sounding statement. As a result, those vision statements trend toward sounding like a marketing slogan, appearing vague, without a time horizon or quantifiable elements, and with little magic to it. Researchers Sooksan Kantabutra and Gayle Avery share what makes a good or even a great vision statement:

> *A leader should espouse a vision that:*
> *– is brief (so that it can be remembered and repeated easily);*
> *– contains a prime goal to be achieved;*
> *– can encompass all organizational interests;*
> *– is not a one-time, specific goal that can be met, and then discarded;*
> *– provides a source of motivation for employees to do their best by including a degree of difficulty or stretch;*
> *– offers a long-term perspective for the organization and indicates the future environment in which it will function;*
> *– is unlikely to be changed by market or technology changes; and is viewed as desirable by employees.*[2]

Trying to hit every item on this entire list can be overwhelming. It might be a big ask of the team to keep all these in mind while at the same time being creative. Let these guidelines inform your vision creation at the start, then dive into the work. Once you have drafted the first version, benchmark it against these guidelines and rework it in cycles. You don't have to tick all the boxes.

Inspire the team with what Harvard sociologist Rosabeth Moss Kanter says about vision: "A vision is not just a picture of what could be; it is an appeal to our better selves, a call to become something more."[3] Kanter's definition appears more philosophical than the empirical, bullet-pointed list from Kantabutra and Avery. What Kanter sees as inflection to stem growth, Kantabutra and Avery describe as a purposeful statement that can aid the organization in the long term. Both see a vision as valuable guidance for any organization.

A vision needs to be specific. A wishy-washy statement is unlikely to speak to your stakeholder groups and inspire action. You need to address your primary stakeholders, keeping their emotional and rational reactions in consideration. In my experience, the sweet spot of a great vision lies where three balanced pairs of elements overlap: heart and brain, detail and aspiration, and purpose and measurability.

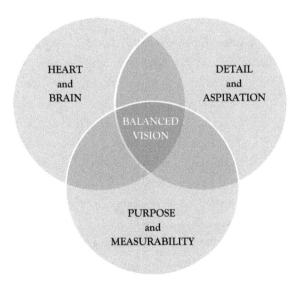

Figure 6.3 The three pairs of a balanced vision

Heart and Brain

A great vision touches your heart *and* brain. Stakeholders should thoroughly understand the vision; this includes clarity about the value you create for your customers. It also means that the vision needs to be relevant. An idea that makes sense but isn't relevant will hardly raise attention, engage people, or inspire action. Addressing stakeholders' rational thinking is probably the more accessible part of crafting a vision statement. I have yet to work with a core team that cannot write a sensible and relevant vision.

But human beings are funny creatures, we have emotions! And these emotions play a huge role in our decision-making process. When a manager somewhere in the middle of your organization sees a new vision for the first time, they don't only have a rational reaction. Hopefully, this manager will also feel something. This depends on how much the core team could charge the vision emotionally. Emotions are crucial in embracing or rejecting a vision. It is just like my favorite author of all time stated:

> *If you want to build a ship, don't drum up the men to gather wood, divide the work and give orders. Instead, teach them to yearn for the vast and endless sea.*
>
> —Antoine de Saint Exupéry

The following anecdote shows how paramount emotional engagement is: A master went to his construction site to find out how the work was going. Arriving there, he saw a bricklayer who looked distant. He came closer and asked: "What are you doing?" The man answered that he was laying bricks. The master kept walking and asked the same question to a second bricklayer, who answered: "I am building a wall." Finally, he noticed a very enthusiastic man who was working with energy and focus. He then asked the same question: "What are you doing?"—"Sir, I am building a cathedral!" It is all about charging what we want to achieve with positive emotions; they fuel our fire.

Remember, from earlier, Wikipedia's vision entailed living in the ideal world, where everyone has access to all human knowledge. It is this vision that motivates countless people to contribute their time, knowledge, and money. People write and review articles in their spare time and make donations to the online encyclopedia. Wikipedia's vision addresses hearts and brains alike.

Which part of their vision statement speaks to your brain? Think about it for a moment. It might be something along the lines of providing free knowledge that you can acquire. Who doesn't like a gift, right? And what is the element touching your heart? You might feel an emotional connection to what free knowledge can trigger: a more equal distribution of opportunities, wealth, health, and peace.

To be clear, emotions don't necessarily have to be positive. Less noble motives can also fuel them. In Nike's formative years, their vision statement was *to destroy Adidas*, capturing a desire to end their unchallenged dominance.[4] I suggest you load a vision with positive emotions, rather than feed from negative terms. I believe that positive emotions—in general, and for a vision in particular—attract a different kind of person than negative emotions, just like Nike's current vision statement: *We see a world where everybody is an athlete—united in the joy of movement.* I'd rather join a business inspiring me to create something than to tear something down.

Detail and Aspiration

Let's check Wikipedia's vision for the second balanced pair of elements. Does it show detail while at the same time being aspirational? The aspiration jumps the eye: contain all human knowledge and make it accessible to everyone, free of charge. It speaks to our noble selves, to make the world a better place, to further democratize the global society by sharing what we have (knowledge), and by providing what is needed to keep it running (money). A vision should be aspirational and evoke a sense of belonging. *This is an endeavor worth participating in. It's something grand and bigger than what I could achieve on my own. I want to be part of that.*

Wikipedia's vision statement is also detailed; it contains footprint (the planet), customers (every single person), and product (sum of all human knowledge). I even suggest their type of business (not-for-profit) and the business model are partly captured in the term *free access*: it indicates a business model that is built on revenue streams other than charging users, for example, advertising or donations, with the latter being the case. In addition, they imply that their chosen market is education. You see, there might be more in it than what we initially read.

Now, there remains one missing detail: a timeframe—it is unclear by when or in which year Wikipedia wants to approximate its vision. In their case, it might be impossible to ever state that all knowledge is captured, given the rate and speed at which humankind increases knowledge. By leaving a timeframe out of their vision statement, Wikipedia meets Kantabutra and Avery's suggestion that a vision "is not a one-time, specific goal that can be met, and then discarded." As a matter of fact, Wikipedia's vision matches all their guidelines listed earlier.

Purpose and Measurability

Sometimes, vision statements are very close to an organization's purpose. Wikipedia's purpose is "to benefit readers by acting as an encyclopedia, a comprehensive written compendium that contains information on all branches of knowledge."[5] Here, the link between purpose and vision is evident. However, this is not always the case. Some of the best vision statements I've seen clients design complied with all guidelines of great visions, but one: a clear link to purpose. Why? Some didn't have a clearly stated purpose in place that they could link a vision to. For other teams, it was so obvious how vision and purpose connected that they forgot to be explicit about it. Just because the core team can make the connection doesn't mean everyone else in an organization can. You want to make sure every stakeholder sees how vision and purpose align. Don't leave it to chance.

What about measurability? The caveat to loading your vision with purpose is that you need to avoid sounding vague. If a vision is too jargon-heavy, then less people will feel that the core team fully understands what they want to achieve. Jargon can easily throw off the fact-oriented rational types in your organization. The antidote: be specific about what you want to achieve. And if you are more the numbers type and feel a little itch you want to scratch, then add concrete figures about *how much* and *by when* you want to achieve the desired picture.

For example, if you run a company in the health care industry, a nondescript vision may state that you *profitably provide life-saving health care logistics to those in need.* If you were to crack down on the details, a highly specific vision would say *doctors and cancer patients trust we deliver life-saving drugs, and by 2025, we will reach U.S.$1.2 billion in turnover, with a 15 percent RoS in the United States and Canada.* I'm not suggesting that *every* part in your vision needs to be backed up by specific numbers. But you should aim to be as specific as possible, finding a balance that feels right. Be mindful about what your organization needs, and your discussion will be headed the right way.

To a certain degree, the art of storytelling might help. According to authors Chip and Dan Heath, what makes messages stick comes down to what they call SUCCESs: simple, unexpected, concrete, credible, emotional, stories.[6] A vision is a message about the future. Reduce it to its most essential components, without reducing its meaning, or dumbing it down. The stickier your vision, the better.

Whatever your vision and strategy might look like in the end, the dominant element should be value creation. It is the most important factor for a company's profitability and long-term success.[7] I'm not talking about shareholder value, but about the value you create for clients consuming your product or service. Value is subjective. What's valuable to your clients might not necessarily be valuable to yourself, while your own definition of value might be irrelevant to your clients. Exploring client needs—and the value they are seeking—is an integral step prior to launching products or services.

Value is what defines a customer's willingness to pay, and the willingness to sell of suppliers and employees.[8] Value can be created on different sides of an exchange, in multiple facets. First, by the value you take home as a business, captured in the form of profit. Second, the value a customer perceives in a transaction with a seller, such as what they receive in exchange for the price they pay. Finally, there is value created for suppliers, for example, when they receive payment or are part of a value chain that is in line with their values.

Is it easy to achieve? Obviously not. Trust in your team and design the vision one step at a time. Benchmark it against the preceding set of guidelines and take it from there. Even if you find yourself working on this vision for a few hours—maybe repeatedly—it is worth the time. We are talking about the future of your organization or the contribution of the unit you lead. Don't rush this. Your vision is what defines all consecutive steps of the strategy design workshop: KPIs and workstreams will be derived from this vision. Therefore, you really want to make sure you achieve an 80 percent complete draft version, at least. Having worked on the vision, we have now come to the second tangible outcome of the workshop: KPIs.

Key Outcome #2: Your Strategic KPI Dashboard to Measure Success

Congratulations! You have created the first tangible outcome of your strategy design workshop. What now? The vision sounds great! It might feel easy to plaster it across your offices and rely on it for the next three years. That can quickly lead to disaster. Admittedly exaggerated, I can imagine you have seen similar behavior at some point in your career: fancy posters displaying something apparently worth displaying, without further context, follow-up, or a link to daily business. This is how vision statements and entire strategy initiatives become jokes between colleagues and eventually disappear. The same is true for purpose statements, corporate values, leadership principles, and more. That's not what you want. Instead of creating posters, foster transparency about where you are at any given moment on your way toward the vision.

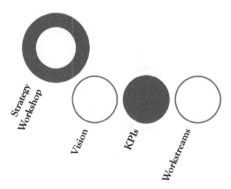

Figure 6.4 Content of a strategy workshop—KPIs

How do you know if you are getting closer to the vision? As they say, what you can't measure you cannot manage. Let's make the vision measurable by designing a dashboard of strategically relevant success indicators, such as KPIs. The aim is to compile a set that will provide an overview of the implementation process. You'll be able to keep track of the direction you're moving in and the progress you're making. As a core team, you define how you measure the organization's strategic performance and whether you are moving closer to the vision.

Deriving these KPIs often depends on the level of analytical skills among the core team members. Some may find it more difficult than others to define a KPI for seemingly intangible elements in your vision. This is the moment for the numbers guys. You start taking the vision apart, element by element, word by word, to identify what you want to measure. Once the team has identified the key elements to be measured, the gold nuggets, you can start talking about concrete KPIs. You will reach the best outcomes when you stay creative and think outside the metaphorical box. You should not limit yourself to KPIs you are familiar with, or which are already in place anyway. Allow a broad discussion about the gold nuggets in your vision and how to measure them. Then decide which of the potential KPIs will make it into your strategy cockpit. Chances are, your vision statement already contains some KPIs, including turnover, growth rate, number of new clients, market position, or similar. These are your low-hanging fruits.

Vision Statement	We are the recognized industry leader (1), providing proactive and effective data-driven service (2). We anticipate and deliver accurate and on-time information, simplifying growing complexity (3) to achieve shared goals and outcomes (4). We enable business success (5) that enhances brand value. We attract, retain and empower the best talent (6) and thrive with a shared purpose (7)—to impact the end users' lives. We have established a new service business model (8).
KPI Dashboard	(1) Third Party external market research, Net Promoter Score (2) Ratio proactive vs reactive activities, customer SLA fulfillment rate (3) Rate of implemented service requirements to simplification (4) Fulfillment rate of contractual commitments, solution uptime (5) Service cost vs sales growth, % of implemented service requirements (6) Retention rate, yearly employee survey (7) Add purpose-related questions to employee survey (8) Revenue from new service business models

Figure 6.5 Work-in-progress example of a vision and KPI dashboard

Low-hanging fruits are often so-called lagging indicators. These tend to change when some event or trend has already happened, for example, an organization's earnings. Once a company's year-end results are calculated, all the events that led to that number lie in the past. Lagging indicators are useful, no doubt. But it's integral to include leading indicators as well, which are sometimes the trickier ones to identify.

Leading indicators change before an event or trend materializes. They are an early warning sign. A leading indicator for a change in earnings could be a strong increase in client complaints. Not dealt with properly, these complaints might turn into frustrations and a change in buying behavior, leading to lower earnings in the future.

At some point, you might feel a bit lost, not knowing how to measure one or the other key element in our vision. If you don't know what to name a certain KPI, just write down what it should tell you or what you want to be able to decide based on it. Give it your best shot and think about who might be able to help. Not every expert will participate in this workshop. Reach out after the session, create a proposal, and then bring it back to the core team's attention.

To decide on the number of KPIs in your strategy cockpit, let's take the example of what controls you have on an electric car's dashboard. Typically, this would include current energy consumption, battery life and reach, current speed limit and actual speed, the temperature inside and outside of the vehicle, headlights, current time, traffic data, and resulting optimal route. This amounts to between 8 and 10 essential elements, the maximum number a driver can keep an eye on while at the same time focusing on the surrounding traffic. The same is true for your strategic dashboard.

Once you have finished the KPI longlist, condense it to no more than 8 to 10. Your longlist might contain significantly more success indicators. I have seen lists of 25 and more potential indicators. Identify KPIs that are useful in measuring more than just one key element in your vision. Other elements might need a combination of various KPIs. A clearcut dashboard will help you stay on top of progress. The dashboard provides focus and clarity and helps you formulate your message to the organization regarding progress. Aim for clarity now, and you will benefit from it once you start communicating and implementing your strategy.

By the end of this step in the strategy design workshop, you will have connected your first key outcome, your vision, with your second key outcome, the KPIs. What you now hold in your hands is:

- A vision statement with highlighted key elements
- A dashboard containing a set of strategic KPIs to keep track of your strategy initiative

Key Outcome #3: Workstreams That Drive You Toward the Vision

If we interpret a vision as the destination you type into your vehicle's GPS, a KPI dashboard is what helps you stay on top of things while driving. The workstreams are the voltage of the electric engine moving you forward. They fuel your strategy initiative, drive your KPIs, and propel you toward the vision.

Strategic workstreams are the priorities in your strategy, describing how you create value. Together with vision and KPIs, workstreams are captured in your strategy map.

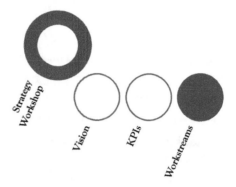

Figure 6.6 Content of a strategy workshop—workstreams

Start defining workstreams by asking your core team to discuss initiatives the organization might need to drive strategic KPIs in the right direction. This is the moment team members have been waiting for. Brace yourself for impact—at this point in the design workshop, the team can easily derail, discussing a wide range of projects they would like to start, on very different levels. It is the moment where they throw in ideas of all kinds, argue for projects already running (which they like), or for killing existing initiatives (which they don't like). They also throw new ideas into the mix that may leave massive room for interpretation, causing discussions that take the group down a rabbit hole. Your role is to help them avoid time-consuming discussions at this stage.

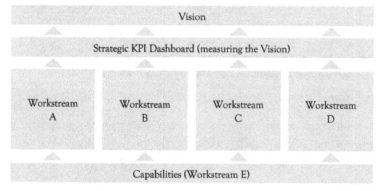

Figure 6.7 Simplified strategy map

Starting Point #1

Ask the team to decide which projects they feel the organization needs to start in order to drive the KPIs. Limit the number of answers to three per person. It will force each individual to make choices and to prioritize.

Starting Point #2

Make the team create a total project inventory listing projects that are already running. Existing initiatives and projects that support your new strategy should be promoted to the status of a strategic project, to increase visibility, remove barriers, and increase support.

Once the team has listed all existing and new projects they feel are needed, they populate the strategy map by arranging and sorting the projects into workstreams. This is a bit of a back-and-forth discussion, creating an understanding of how different projects are connected, how they might depend on each other, and how they should be logically grouped.

In this context, let's talk about funding and budget. If an existing project is not strategically relevant, consider defunding it. Stop anything that drains your resources; you will need everything you have to reach your vision. Every resource that you invest in pet projects is not available for strategy implementation. This is about focus and rigor.

In the context of their strategy process, a business-to-business (B2B) company redefined the ideal type of client they wanted to serve. Among others, one characteristic was that any new client needed to be large enough to potentially cross a minimum annual revenue threshold, which would make them a Type A account. The core team reviewed the existing client portfolio and began benchmarking each client against these characteristics. As a result, the company identified a handful of existing clients that would qualify as Type A. They wanted to double the revenue with these clients over the coming three years.

To achieve this goal, the company couldn't simply staff their key account teams with new hires. The resources needed to come from within the organization. To free up these resources, the core team decided to reduce the service levels for all other clients, those who wouldn't qualify as Type A. After a heated debate, the team agreed to terminate field sales efforts for Type B accounts and to merge several client-specific in-house sales teams into a newly installed client center, pooling Type B and Type C clients. In addition, they agreed that contracts with Type B accounts would not be broadened beyond the current scope of service, nor would they renew contracts with Type C accounts.

You can imagine how intense the discussions were between the core team members. Reaching this agreement was a breakthrough moment. However, the sales leader wasn't fully on board with the decision. He had initially acquired most Types B and C clients and had close relationships with them. In the following months, the sales leader did not reduce the Types B and C business as agreed, holding up resources from transitioning toward serving Type A clients. As a result, the company didn't have the necessary capacity on Type A accounts and failed to reach the financial goals laid out in their strategy.

Successful strategy is all about bringing clarity to the organization. It's important to prioritize. By the end of your workstream discussion, you should have a clear answer to these questions:

- What are our three to five strategic priorities?
- What projects sit inside these workstreams?
- How does each project and each workstream drive the strategic KPIs?
- Which of these workstreams might be more urgent than others?

The people you will ask to implement workstreams typically will have a full work schedule already. Strategy implementation often means additional topics to drive and to take care of. Your organization is not likely to embrace your strategy if it means adding a pile of work onto an employee's existing pile of work. Help people identify what they can let go, to make space for strategically relevant efforts.

People and budgets are typically maxed out even before a strategy project starts. The implication for you as a leader is that you need to be mindful about the expectations you create. Instead of concerning the organization, help the core team become crystal clear on the significance of each workstream. The sequence and timeframe of implementation are crucial to avoid overburdening the organization. It might not necessarily be a topic for the design workshop. But it certainly will become a topic when you discuss budget allocation. Ask yourself which workstreams should be prioritized and park the rest for now.

There are some essential questions you should ask during a strategy design workshop:

- Are we crystal clear about who our customers are?
- Which elements in the strategy will ensure that our customers see the unique value in our offering?
- What is the value they perceive from choosing our offering over the competition?

It is not enough if your strategy claims you will be the best, the first, or the fastest at something. That might sound aspirational, but it misses the point. The commercial value of your strategy will be determined by how your customers will benefit from it. If you realize at any point in the design process that you are not explicit about the commercial value proposition of your strategy, go back to your vision. Check whether it addresses purpose, impact, and commercial value.

By the end of the strategy design workshop, you will be holding a draft version of your strategy, consisting of a vision statement, a KPI dashboard, and workstreams. What you now want to make sure is that the team is clear on the next steps.

- What do we communicate about the strategy process now, and to whom?
- How does the strategy process continue? What are the next steps? When do we meet again?
- Who takes the interim lead for which workstream? Who follows up on what?

Once you've answered these questions, you are ready for some serious work in Step 4 of the strategy process: refinement.

Identity Refinement Phase

Outcome: Organizational identity and strategy ready for implementation.

Participants: Strategy core team, additional internal and external experts, PMO.

Length: A few weeks to several months, depending on the scope of the initiative and the size of the organization.

Standard: Before you start implementing, make sure you've created the organizational intent, or it will come back and bite you, I promise.

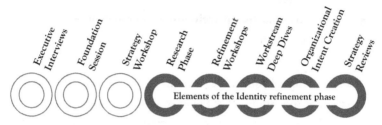

Figure 6.8 Elements of the identity refinement phase

The largest part of work during a refinement phase is about amplifying the strategy. However, the remaining elements of organizational identity you have designed should not be forgotten. It's the phase in which you start testing purpose, values, and behavioral guidelines. Leadership principles or a code of conduct might still need significant attention. I don't want to create the impression that finalizing these elements needs minor effort—often there is *significant* work involved. Nevertheless, I will focus more on the strategic elements of identity in this chapter.

Step 4: Research Phase

After the design workshop, you can successfully move into the refinement phase. One of the first tasks here is to do strategy-related research. The core team will dig into questions that were raised during the design workshop. The aim is to inform your decision making and remove as many of the unknown variables as possible. You will gather facts to remove assumptions. You will potentially:

- Analyze your competitive position
- Map value drivers
- Review your product portfolio
- Study the maturity of your market and understand trends

- Identify your core competencies
- Segment your customers and map the customer journey
- Explore your value chain
- Dismantle your cost structure
- Understand where you make and where you lose money

There are tons of established analysis methods available to help you successfully conduct your research, such as Porter's Five Forces Framework, Blue Ocean Strategy, SWOT, and Growth-Share. This is the ideal time to reach out to experts inside and outside of your organization, conduct interviews, and run surveys. At this stage, involving consultants is usually a way to increase speed and quality of outcomes. Business consultancies are available on relatively short notice to ramp up your resources. They help with analysis work by using expert knowledge, inside and cross-industry.

However, it's essential that you always remain in the driver's seat, with your core team steering the consultants, not the other way around. It is a question of ownership and accountability. You want your core team to own the strategy. If they perceive a loss of leadership in the process, the strategy can quickly become a beast that the team starts to reject.

You want to avoid your team referring to the initiative as the consultancy's strategy. Consultants can't possibly have the same emotional connection to your purpose, desired impact, and values. From their perspective, a certain decision might make little commercial sense, whereas it makes perfect sense to you, based on the full picture of your organizational identity.

There is one more organizational tool you should consider during the research phase. Depending on the size of your organization, choose appropriate software to support your implementation efforts. These tools are designed to make your life easier and your identity implementation more successful, measurable, and trackable. The times when identity initiatives and strategy programs were managed in spreadsheets are over.

I vividly remember how painstaking it was to create monthly board reports, when I was a strategy PMO manager. Merging project planning software, presentation software, and spreadsheets, and then linking them through plugins to create reports. It was complicated, time-consuming, and error-prone.

Fast forward, and you find yourself in the 2020s. There are online tools available for designing and executing strategies. This includes tracking, reporting, and visualization of results, as a basis for better decision making. Some tools have built-in features to support collaboration during the design phase, both within the core team, with additional colleagues, and with external partners. Choose a tool that is flexible enough, especially to adjust to the terminology you are used to, and to support the strategic analyses of your choice.

These applications can help you structure strategic plans from scratch, assign goals to teams and individuals, create status updates, and pull reports. Whichever tool you choose, make sure it helps you work smarter, not harder. The tool should be easy to use, offer state-of-the-art IT security, and should offer a proper API with software and apps you are already using.

Step 5: Refinement Workshops

Once you've completed most of your research, gather the core team to discuss the findings. Invite additional experts if needed to help you understand trends or to interpret market data. In addition, consider pulling together a group of people that have not yet been involved, and ask them to challenge the quality of your work results. This allows you to road-test the draft of your organization's identity, particularly the strategy piece, by hitting it with specific *what-if* scenarios.

These scenarios will stress-test the agility of strategy, for example, if unforeseen circumstances arise. These can be premortems to understand what could potentially sink your strategy and which circumstances would help it thrive. Testing may expose risks, such as a strong reliance on a few key individuals, aging technologies, or a strategy built on wishful thinking rather than facts.

Based on the results and discussions, start refining your strategy: finalize your vision statement, adjust the strategic KPI dashboard, and streamline your workstreams. You might need more than one meeting to achieve all this. But you will realize that this is time very well invested. Also, it can be genuinely energizing work as you see the future emerge in front of your eyes.

The more clarity your core team achieves, the better you will be able to translate strategic goals into individual targets later in the process. Everyone in an organization, individual contributors and leaders alike, must understand how their roles support strategy implementation. Your identity will only flourish if leaders are able to translate strategy into action, by linking it to daily jobs.

In a refinement workshop, the core team spends significant time bringing workstream charters to life. These charters are the interface between strategy and operations—the core team operationalizes strategy by capturing everything that should be part of a workstream, like existing and new projects. They bring them into a logical order, laying out scope and outcomes, and agreeing on milestones and timelines. Furthermore, they create transparency about the degree to which workstreams drive strategic KPIs. A comprehensive charter should capture the following aspects:

- The necessity of the workstream: It captures your current reality, outlining why you need a specific strategic workstream, addressing any existing gaps, and closing stress points. This is not about solutions but about acknowledging what needs fixing.
- The definition of *done*: A description of the results that a workstream will produce, an end goal. It describes the ideal situation after the completion of the workstream.
- SMART goals: A detailed description of workstream goals, such as a breakdown of the definition of done. SMART stands for specific, measurable, action-oriented, realistic, and time-bound.
- Milestones: Intermediate milestones to be achieved, to produce the expected workstream results. Typically, it takes a few milestones to complete a SMART goal.
- Strategic KPIs: A list of KPIs that the workstream influences, and to which degree. This links back to the KPI dashboard in your strategy map and captures the contribution of a workstream to achieving the vision.
- Project inventory: A list of projects that belong to the workstream. Understand where projects fit in and give them the visibility they need—or discontinue them.
- Dependencies: Links to other workstreams and projects. Workstreams typically overlap to a certain degree, with real-world consequences for the people involved. Be clear about the overlaps and collaboration needed.

- Team members, leader, and main stakeholders: Names of individuals, not departments or organizational functions. These are the people that drive a workstream forward and include stakeholders critical to its success.
- Risks and mitigation: A high-level what-if scenario in case certain risks materialize. This does not include time and budget; at this point, your priorities are clear, and thus, you will channel resources where you need them.
- Timeline: Expected timeline to implement a workstream, ideally comprising the high-level timelines of the projects it contains.

Why we need this workstream	Definition of done		
• Which pain points does this workstream alleviate? • Why is removing these pain points urgent and important? • Focus on WHY we need this workstream as opposed to WHAT should be achieved • Describe the rationale for the workstream using findings of your strategy process until this point.	• How will the result of this workstream look once implemented? • What is it that the workstream will achieve? • What are the tangible and intangible result that you want to see? • How does this support the WHY (box to the left)		
Goals	**Milestones**		
• List and describe all goals of the workstream in detail • Make goals SMART, i.e., specific, measurable, action-oriented, realistic, time-bound • Formulate goals, not activities or tasks that need to be performed—for example: "Increase sales by 12 percent in all three key markets" is an activity. Instead formulate the goal: "By end of Q3 2022, sales have increased by at least 12 percent in our three key markets" • Add page if needed	**Short Term**	**Mid Term**	**Long Term**
	• What are the short-term (within a year) milestones leading toward achieving your SMART goals? • Formulate milestones, not activities or tasks that need to be performed	• What are the midterm (1–2 years) milestones leading toward achieving your SMART goals? • Formulate milestones, not activities or tasks that need to be performed	• What are the longer-term (>2 years) milestones leading toward achieving your SMART goals? • Formulate milestones, not activities or tasks that need to be performed

Figure 6.9 Page 1 of a workstream charter manual

Depending on your strategy initiative's complexity, make sure you stay on the right level of detail in your charters. The core team's responsibility is not to take over the project management from those leading existing projects. However, it's imperative that those calling the shots understand the strategic relevance and stakes of their projects, and that there might be further alignment or adjustments to make. Refining the scope and clarifying links to other workstreams or projects may be necessary.

Be precise when formulating different sections in a charter. Highlight milestones and SMART goals to set precedence. For example: *Establishing new reporting standards for sales channels* is neither a goal nor a milestone but is written as an activity. As a SMART goal, it could look like this: *New reporting standards for all sales channels are established by the end of the third quarter of 2025, in our European and North American branches, and by the end of the first quarter of 2026, in all remaining operations.* Make sure you formulate the breakdown of each SMART goal into milestones in a similarly rigorous way.

I am explicit about properly formulating workstreams because they are the starting point for putting strategy into action. Action means reallocating resources toward strategically relevant work. The more rigorously you prioritize and pace your goals, the more successfully your initiative will trickle down the business and manifest into individual targets.

Step 6: Workstream Deep Dive Sessions

These sessions aim to finish the workstream charters before having the core team challenge and scrutinize the strategy map in a final review. The workstream leader gathers their team to add as much quality detail to the charter. The session should be conducted in iterative cycles over a few weeks, with the group researching additional information between sessions. Besides bringing as much life as possible into a charter, capture open questions for the core team, for discussion and decision making. If this type of work is new to the team, especially the leader, support the workstream team with a resource already familiar with the process. This external or internal strategy facilitator aids in formulating each section of the charter, seamlessly linking the sections, and assists in reaching the appropriate level of detail and accuracy.

Proper workstream formulation takes time. Even if pressure is high and deadlines are tight, nothing good comes from rushing things. I've seen time and again teams starting with a brilliant idea, and instead of doing their research and properly mapping out a workstream, they think they will figure it out on the fly. That is a dangerous approach to strategy design as other workstreams might depend on you. If later in the process the entire rollout stalls because of wishy-washy workstream creation, you might need to start again from scratch.

At the end of the deep dive sessions, and after answering open questions, the work is handed back to the core team for final review and endorsement. Last briefings and reviews might happen in a separate meeting before starting to create an organizational intent document.

Step 7: Organizational Intent Document

Now that you have formulated various elements of your organizational identity, you're in need of a document that captures your initiative. It should outline every element of identity that you have created until this point, including your impact statement, principles, mission, vision, and strategy map. While writing this outline, you may realize how far you've come—it may be time to consolidate the output. This is a crucial preparation step for your communication efforts, to transform the organization and enable your people to live the new identity. But right now, many of the work results are likely to be in different formats, electronic or paper-based, stored on different drives, and some might only exist in the heads of those involved up until now.

Writing your organizational intent helps you crystalize your thinking and understand whether the story it tells makes sense end-to-end. The document should have flowing text with supporting visuals, rather than bullet-point lists. It needs to leave little to no room for interpretation. It will become your go-to document, the one source of truth for anything around your identity. Try to avoid jargon as much as possible.

Don't use fancy words that might sound important. Flowery or expert-level vocabulary have their place but won't necessarily help your organization understand the message you want to convey.

Composing an intent document can be a collaborative effort of core team members supported by a PMO manager and by a communications manager. The table of contents of an organizational intent document includes:

Section 1—Introduction and Rationale

Link it to the results of the foundation session, research phase, executive interviews, potential clients survey results, and so on. It outlines the status quo of your organization and describes the challenges ahead. Reading this chapter, people will see the need and reason for a new identity. Chapters include:

- What the document captures and its intended use
- Challenges of the past few years
- Current reality and status quo of the organization
- Changes and challenges over the coming years
- Unique strengths of the organization

Section 2—The New Identity

This section is about the new organizational identity itself, describing it verbally and with supporting visuals. Structure the section along the Nine Elements of Organizational Identity and explain each element to a level of detail that eliminates as much ambiguity as possible. Create the links between the elements and how they support each other. Chapters include:

- Purpose and impact
- Values and behavioral guidelines

- Mission
- Vision
- Strategy map
- Overarching goals
- Individual targets
- Capability building
- Management systems

Section 3—Implementation Approach

This part outlines governance, timelines, budgets, and the role of individual contributors and leaders.

- Roadmap, prioritization, and timelines
- Budget allocation
- Role of the leadership population and individual contributors
- What's in it for me?
- Speed and mindset
- Communication and transparency
- Governance

Not all information is for everyone. Some details, especially in your strategy, might be confidential and should not be disclosed. That is your judgment call.

An organizational intent document, especially strategic workstream charters and strategy maps, depicts a snapshot of the present and the desired future, and as such, it is static. Once you finish writing your organizational intent, freeze it, figuratively speaking, along with the workstream charters. It is not designed to track progress. When you start moving your identity into action, use proper project management tools to steer the implementation of your initiative.

Step 8: Strategy Review Sessions

While your identity contains permanent elements such as purpose, impact, and principles, your strategy is more of a moving target. Even your vision might not be immune to change. Remember the car GPS analogy? As the vision is comparable to a destination, the strategy is the way toward the destination. What is true for road traffic also applies to strategy. Sometimes you need to take a detour, sometimes you can detect a short cut, sometimes a route needs adjusting. Your organization is part of an environment that is constantly moving, changing, even transforming. In the same context, you should regularly test your strategy for validity, including your vision and workstreams. I suggest this be done at least twice a year.

Testing the continued validity of your strategy is different to checking on the implementation status. Strategy review sessions are about effectiveness; about asking whether you are still doing the right things. These regular reviews ensure that you stay sharp, and course correct as needed. Technological leaps, new players, the bankruptcy of a competitor, changes in the regulatory environment—to name just a few potential inflection points—will put your strategy to the test and might require fast adjustments to seize opportunities along the way. Even without facing these specific major events, testing your strategy should be a regular check-in during the implementation phase.

During these sessions, take a step back, broaden your view, and seek out the bigger picture. Take a helicopter perspective and detach yourself from the details of your strategy. Ask questions to help you objectively assess whether you are still on the right track. Look for changes to external factors, based on your SWOT analysis, that may pose a risk to the strategy. Seek out the solutions to mitigate potential risks. Check whether your vision is still ambitious enough. Let your PMO gather intelligence beforehand to fuel a powerful discussion with the core team. Don't be afraid to adjust your strategy and communicate these adjustments.

Part 2 Executive Summary

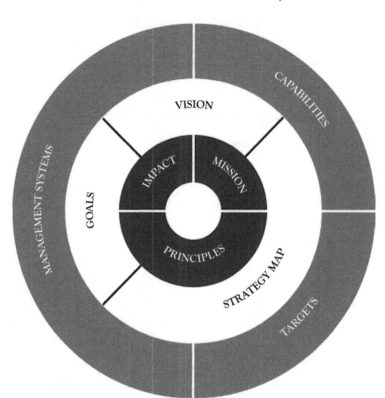

The Nine Elements of Organizational Identity

On my website, I provide a *field guide* to support your strategy and identity process. The guide helps you bring the process outlined in this book to life in your business. The field guide for this book contains:

- Questionnaire for executive interviews
- Questions to explore your unique strengths and challenges
- Exercise description to formulate your mission
- Exercise to identify your desired impact
- Ways to capture your values and behavioral guidelines
- Exercise to draft your vision statement
- Exercise to derive a strategic KPI dashboard
- Worksheet and manual for strategic workstreams
- Template to capture vision, KPI dashboard, and workstreams

- Template and manual for organizational intent
- Checklist for the research phase

Access the field guide at https://brueckmann.ca/fieldguide

Questions to Explore

Mind-Setting

- What is the legacy you want to leave behind? Are you clear about your individual purpose and values?
- How conscious are the leaders on your team, and which mindsets are at play?
- How comfortable is the leadership team to challenge and be challenged?
- Are your team development efforts embedded in the strategy design?

Foundation

- What are the unique strengths of our organization?
- What are the key challenges over the coming years?
- What is the higher purpose and desired impact of our organization—beyond transactional benefits?
- Which diamond values define and inform individual and organizational behavior?
- What does our organization do, and for whom?

Strategy

- Is our strategy design embedded in an overarching identity design?
- Do we have proper foresight to inform our strategic planning process?
- Is our vision balanced, addressing the three pairs—heart and brain, detail and aspiration, purpose and measurability?

- Does our KPI dashboard track the progress for all key elements of our vision?
- Which workstreams propel us toward achieving the vision?
- Are the goals of our workstreams SMART?
- Do we understand how different workstreams and goals depend on each other?

Refinement

- Have we tested and refined purpose/impact, principles, and mission so that they are *good enough*?
- Have we fine-tuned our strategy map with vision, KPIs, and workstreams, based on proper research of assumptions?
- Which software will we choose to support collaboration and to make identity implementation more flexible and transparent?
- Have we consolidated the organizational identity design process into an organizational intent document?

PART 3

Empowering Organizations to Implement Identity

In 2008, I visited Cuba for the first time. Backpacking across the country, we used every opportunity to mingle with locals and immerse ourselves in real Cuban life. Some of the most striking memories of this trip were a widespread shortage of goods and the worn state of many buildings. It was the year Fidel Castro handed power to his brother Raúl, before the government slowly introduced reforms to improve the economic situation of Cubans. On the outside—and inside—of many buildings, we noticed structures made of lumber and planks to support walls, preventing them from collapsing. These weren't some abandoned shacks but houses and buildings that occupied families. These structures initially looked a lot like the building scaffoldings I was familiar with.

Looking at them more closely, I realized that there was a difference between these support structures and the scaffoldings I was used to seeing in more developed countries (apart from not being made from wood). The scaffoldings I had seen before were temporary in nature, used to erect a building. The structures in Cuba were permanent. They stabilized existing buildings while also providing scaffolding for repair workers. But it wasn't until years later that I understood the power of metaphoric scaffoldings for strategy and identity implementation.

Support structures of organizations are made up of systems, procedures, and governing bodies. They often maintain and support the status quo—not the change. To avoid that an organization hinders its very own change efforts, it must remove all barriers and empower broad-based action.[1] Barriers can be organizational, such as processes and structures. They can be human: leaders or individual contributors sabotaging our efforts. Combined, they present a perfect storm.

In this part, I provide guidance on how to create a support structure for your initiative, enabling a successful rollout of strategy and identity. Rest assured, the three remaining elements of organizational identity are as important for success as the strategy itself. In fact, it is very unlikely that you will reap the fruits of your work if you disregard targets, capabilities, and management systems. You're about to see why these three elements are the scaffolding that holds identity in place.

CHAPTER 7

Sorry Coach

Individual Targets Make the Difference

In my adolescent years, my football coach taught me a lesson about targets that I only understood later in life. I was one of the top scorers on the team, yet the coach benched me for several matches. He would rather accept defeat than let me play. Even worse, he wouldn't tell me why he benched me. Over time, I realized that it was kind of his jam. He hardly ever gave us clear instructions or a game plan. We were just a lousy team without a playbook or leadership. We didn't know what he expected of us as a team, let alone of individual players. We knew our roles but were unclear about specific contributions and how those were supposed to come together. So, when the coach finally let me play again, I was confused and anxious that he would arbitrarily bench me again. He set no targets to aim for, and I didn't know how he wanted me to contribute to the team's success, beyond scoring.

Side note: football is a sport where you kick a ball with your foot, hence the name. If you live in North America, you might have a different sport that comes to mind, played largely with hands and an egg-shaped ball: American football, or as I like to call it, handegg. I had to set the records straight. Just take the hit.

Targets Make Contributions Visible

Everyone can contribute to implementing aspects of the identity once they know how. We can derive individual targets—both qualitative and quantitative—from overarching strategic goals. For example, we break

down revenue goals into markets or product categories, and then assign individual quotas to sales teams and every individual.

Formulating targets is highly relevant for strategy implementation and the success of your identity initiative. Deriving targets is operational work for leaders and involves breaking down bigger, strategic goals into smaller, actionable targets. If you don't derive individual targets from your strategy, you are robbing people of the opportunity to contribute to the success of your business meaningfully.

Those leading a strategy program sometimes forget that the vast majority of people in their organization potentially haven't yet heard of the new strategy, let alone resonate with the identity. On the contrary, the core team has, by this point, had so much exposure to these topics that they want to stop talking and start implementing. They start pushing the organization forward and sometimes become displeased with what they perceive as slow progress. But an organization needs time to understand, accept, and adapt to change. I vividly remember an impatient CEO telling their core team that they had enough of the talk, demanding fast results. The CEO wanted the strategy topic off their desk to make space for other pressing issues. After realizing they were out of sync with the rest of the business, they agreed on a proper communication and implementation plan that helped large parts of the company understand and support the new strategy.

Helping the organization to make sense of a new identity is a vital step before implementation can start. You might oversee the initiative, but your organization will help bring it to life. And to do so, you want to help them first understand it, rationally. Then you want to help your people realize what's expected of them, how their roles might change, and what's in it for them personally. Only then will employees embrace a new organizational identity emotionally and help drive it.

Here is where strategically relevant targets make all the difference, and where the magic happens. Targets are role specific and range depending on a job description and responsibilities. If leaders throughout an organization can help every individual understand what and why they need to do things differently, and then help them reshape the focus of their daily work, they align all forces. People start pulling in one orchestrated direction, unleashing the organization's full potential.

In my experience, leaders fail to translate strategy into action for two main reasons. First, there is not enough dialog within an organization about identity or strategy. People aren't aware of it because they haven't received enough information, let alone had a chance to ask questions to understand the relevance for them personally. In other words, there is not enough communication happening to entice further employee engagement.

The other reason strategy is not easily translated into action is that leaders don't know how to break strategic goals into individual targets. Maybe they have never done it before or don't understand the strategic goals themselves, especially if they were not involved during the strategy design phase. The issue is that this exercise typically falls down the cracks when strategy consultants leave an organization and no one within the organization catches the ball. If an organization lacks knowledge on how to formulate strategically relevant targets, the odds are that they either struggle in doing so or don't realize the importance in the first place—and don't ever try.

This is the moment when your initiative suddenly experiences the laws of physics; as a result of a loss of airflow, it falls out of the sky. In this analogy, your entire organization is the passengers. You better make sure the airflow is steady and the momentum high.

When you break goals into targets, ensure you focus on qualitative and quantitative targets. Strategic goals in your strategy map might be relatively easy to develop quantitatively. Let's say you are a manufacturer of heavy commercial vehicles. Trucks collect tons of data through sensors that they regularly send back to you, such as road conditions, weather, tire pressure, or the weight of the load. Now imagine a strategic workstream that tackles the monetization of that data. A goal of the workstream could sound like this: "By the end of next year, we see annual revenues of at least $500 million stemming from business models based on vehicle data."

Just think about the playing field this goal opens. Based on the scope of the workstream, this goal will potentially touch many people across departments, which all need to deliver their contributions to meet the goal. Individual contributions should be transparently derived from the overall strategic plan and captured in a performance management system. Combined with the right type of leadership, this will tremendously increase the odds of the workstream delivering the expected results. Make it measurable, and you can manage it.

Targets Help Build a Culture of Justice and Accountability

I have a rule of thumb for breaking down goals into targets. Rather than measuring and controlling your organization to an unhealthy degree by tracking every detail, ask yourself which 20 percent of the measures, actions, and targets will make 80 percent of the difference. In strategy implementation, I would always argue that 80 percent is good enough to start with, especially when it comes to time-consuming strategy controlling and reporting. Ensure you assess which information you need— and then manage those targets precisely.

Produce controlling and reporting to accelerate your organization, to show momentum and demonstrate progress, to celebrate successes, and thus facilitate more change. Don't install reporting to control your organization's every move, avoid mistakes, or because you don't trust your strategy. If these are driving motivators, there is something in the water. It signifies an environment lacking trust, positive conflict, and accountability.

Goals and targets provide an excellent opportunity to reinforce a desired culture. Aligning people around collective goals can help tear down barriers and build bridges between formerly isolated organizational silos. The right leadership and performance culture will be more valuable to a successful strategy implementation than any reporting and controlling will ever be.

Where inspiring leadership and a healthy culture are missing, a detailed controlling and reporting system will only lead to people playing the system. No matter what the numbers look like, people will find ways to *reach* targets. Where there's a systemic issue in place, no controlling system will help you implement your strategy.

People lie, deceive, and cheat if they fear being punished or mistreated for not reaching targets. I once had an unpleasant discussion with a highly versed corporate controller. Given her experience with how management tended to use findings to blame and condemn, her thoughts weren't about creating transparency with her calculations. She asked me what the result of her calculations should show and wanted to know the desired numbers. She would rather engineer a report to keep management off her back than justify her approach. I leave it to you to judge how likely you feel a strategic initiative can be successful in such an environment.

To avoid undesirable behaviors, harness a culture of justice and accountability. If people feel that targets are set and measured fairly, they don't have any reason to manipulate and play the system to get ahead. Giving people recognition, by publicly celebrating their successes, should be the means of choice. When people see that their contributions are valued, they will likely go the extra mile because they want to, not because they fear the repercussions if they don't.

Not Every Target Is a Number

While strategy-related targets might be measured quantitatively, other elements of your identity might translate better into qualitative targets. Let's take principles, which capture values and behavioral guidelines.

Your identity creation might result in a new or updated code of conduct. It could include desired behaviors regarding diversity, equity, inclusion, and topics related to the integrity of individuals or the organization, from conflicts of interest to being a law-abiding corporation. A code of conduct, however, is not the final result—it is a means to an end. Leaders still need to help their teams translate a guideline into expectations, including distinct behaviors in relevant situations.

Let's look at a real-life example. In their code of conduct, the Swiss company Roche addresses the topic of business integrity wherein, "The terms and conditions that determine the appropriate behavior in business must be assessed on a case-by-case basis by taking into consideration the relevant parameters of each individual case."[1] That means business integrity will look differently depending on a team's cultural background, the legal and regulatory environment of the country they operate in, or the subject matter a department deals with. Translating business integrity into target behaviors for a team of corporate lawyers in Japan will have a different outcome than for a sales team in Chile.

Leaders must help their teams understand and translate principles into desired behaviors within their daily context. This is where principles come to life and provide meaningful guidance to employees.

Targets Are the Basis for Performance Reviews

The outcomes of performance reviews are often the basis for promotions or pay raises. People generally focus on what will help them climb the ranks, get a raise, or avoid trouble. If you don't successfully translate your strategy into individual targets, people will forget about the strategy. Remember: organizations don't implement the strategy; people do. So, it's necessary that everyone understands their targets and how they connect to strategic goals. You create a key ingredient to establish a performance culture: accountability for both the targets and how you meet them.

The pathway to reach your target should be as important as reaching them in the first place. If the way toward reaching a target is flawed, healthy cultures reward digging for root causes and solving the underlying problem. If the process is as significant as the results, leaders provide incentives to do things the right way. They foster honesty and take away reasons to cheat, lie, or deceive to hit targets.

Missing performance standards might result in a negative review. Replace untransparent, gut-feeling-based judgments and decisions with fair systems and processes that are easily accessible. Writing strategy-related targets into performance plans is useless, when leaving people clueless about how to reach them. That would be frustrating and likely trigger disengagement.

When people perceive review processes as fair and understand targets, they can deal with the disappointment of missing them. Leaders should follow up on negative performance reviews with targeted support to help their teams avoid running into failure repeatedly and to accelerate positive development. This requires supportive leaders who know how to translate overarching goals into individual targets and how to make contributions visible.

My football coach was a particularly prominent example of how not to do it. He simply didn't have the capabilities needed to coach. *It's just a youth team*, you might think. Not a big deal. Well, the deal was bigger than I initially realized. After I was continuously benched, I wasn't the only one who started to change their attitude. Some team members began showing up late for games, even with hangovers. Many of us began smoking cigarettes while driving to away games, in the coach's car, with him driving. We gave a horrible picture and got poorly beaten by opposing teams. For a while, I even lost my passion for the game. Targets matter. Understanding your contribution matters. Without them, it cost us our season.

CHAPTER 8

Don't Call Them Soft

Critical Capabilities That Are Hard to Master

CFO asks CEO: What happens if we invest in the development of our people, and then they leave us?
CEO: What happens if we don't, and they stay?

This hypothetical conversation has been shared on social media millions of times.

What happens if you don't invest in the development of your people, and they stay, is this: some will do what they can to keep up with the pace of change around them, maybe by doing more of what they have been doing. Some will self-teach out of curiosity and because they enjoy learning. Some others will hopefully seek out new skills relevant to supporting the implementation of a new identity. Another group will realize that their environment is changing and that they will likely need to learn new capabilities. They may not know where to start or which skills to focus on. Unfortunately, most people will sit and wait.

The silent majority, you might find, are neither against building new skills nor keen on leading the way. They will learn, if they need to, to keep their jobs. But really, they would rather preserve the status quo. They often continue doing what they are familiar with, which falls within their comfort zone. And that is just human nature.

The bottom line is that if you don't invest in the development of your staff, they will likely disengage with the organization's identity or start rebelling against it. The first group feels they lack support for building the necessary skills to succeed in their expected roles and meet their targets.

It leaves them frustrated, and morale will decrease. They won't care about the new strategy or identity anymore, will ignore communications regarding the topic, skip town hall meetings, and avoid the case wherever they can—because they feel it is happening to them, not with them.

Others will see that they need capabilities different from those that made them successful in the past. They realize learning is the only option to remain relevant and deliver value to the organization in the future. They are willing to develop the necessary skills and apply them in their daily work.

Call yourself lucky if you have these rebels in your organization. They care and, because of that, will become vocal. Their driving force is caring for clients, colleagues, and relationships. Mainly, they prioritize what is best for the business and their careers. Another factor that drives is fear. Employees will fear losing their edge, becoming irrelevant, and losing their jobs. And they might come across as a bit rebellious, loud, or slightly aggressive. As long as they raise their voices, you should listen to them. When those who care become silent, you might be in a dangerous place.

The good news is that vocal employees can even compensate for bad leadership. In the ideal world, every leader in an organization would ask themselves which capabilities their teams need to support a new identity. This is a starting point for a dialog with other leaders, and HR, to discuss options for learning and development to acquire essential skills. But if leaders aren't conscious about the needs of their teams—and their areas for development, too—they will only hear the teams screaming the loudest. My message is that you cannot rely on the maturity, consciousness, and self-awareness of your leaders or staff, you need to be a forward-thinker. Therefore, capability development must be integral to your strategy and identity design from the very beginning.

With Capability Building, Strategy Will Thrive

If you design a strategy without questioning the necessary competencies to bring it to life, the chances are you won't get far. Capability development is a core ingredient of identity. Your staff's skills need to be at the center of attention and belong at the heart of strategy. Ask yourself who will execute your strategy and implement your organizational identity.

It is neither the core team nor the organization. In the end, it's the people within the organization who make or break your efforts, the leaders and associates. It's essential that they acquire the critical skills, enabling them to help steer your ship in the right direction.

Investments in capability building are a strategic investment. Rather than relying on what you already know, ask yourself what you need to learn to best address the challenges you face. An organization's ability to develop relevant capabilities has a direct impact on financial performance, customer success, and employee satisfaction.[1] About 90 percent of companies know that they have a significant skill gap emerging in the years to come. Only 16 percent believe that they know how to close it. What's even more shocking is that 60 percent of these organizations say that their learning and development (L&D) budget has no specific connection to their strategic business goals.[2] Let that sink in. They admit to consciously throwing money out of the window. It will likely get worse, without knowing how to close the skill gap.

It is a consequence of business leaders not acknowledging the importance of continuous L&D. A lack of interest and engagement leads to L&D becoming a siloed HR topic with little connection to business needs. While HR might be doing everything they can, they still miss the mark because they are not partnering with business leaders to identify the strategic skill gaps and a way of filling them. Business leaders should raise some tough questions: Which capabilities do we need to drive value for the business? How do we acquire those capabilities through up-skilling, training, and hiring? How do we assess and transform our approach to skill building and training? How can we reposition the L&D function as a true partner to the business to achieve that?

The first step is addressing these questions. Enable HR and L&D functions to learn some critical skills themselves and become true partners of the business. This includes the ability to understand their organization's business model, the numbers involved, and how to speak the business language, rather than L&D or HR speak. HR should prove to the business that capability building and closing the skill gap have a return on investment.

If HR can implement L&D opportunities to the business at an eye level, Step 2 becomes possible. They will be able to partner with the business and identify the strategic capability gaps. As a result, they adjust the training environment, engage senior leaders to showcase the importance of learning, and stop flushing money down the toilet for nonessential training. This includes letting go of nice-to-have training or pet projects if they don't hold up in a strategic skill gap assessment and a subsequent refresh of the training and development environment.

Business leaders and L&D need to partner for success; otherwise, they're both doomed. Overcoming the divide between the business and HR or L&D functions can be challenging. L&D teams often lack business focus or don't feel competent enough. They shy away from discussions about the return on investment of training and learning. At the same time, business leaders aren't consulting with L&D. Instead, they decide on training their teams to the best of their ability, bypassing L&D. These leaders, however, aren't necessarily skilled enough to identify the strategic capabilities they should invest in, and usually miss the mark. They unintentionally waste resources and frustrate their people when they realize down the road that the time they invested in acquiring skills was in vain because these new skills don't help them live up to expectations.

Closing the Strategic Capability Gap

Hopefully you're well aware of existing skill gaps in your business or know where to anticipate gaps in the near future. To close these gaps, I recommend you take these four steps:

1. Assess whether you can conduct a proper capability gap analysis internally, through a qualitative examination identifying the skills needed to fill the gap. If you lack experience, partner with external consultants who have a proven track record in linking capability building to business strategy.

2. Based on the gap analysis results, re-evaluate your existing L&D measures in place, including on-the-job and classroom training, job rotation, and others. Identify and preserve the measures that help you fill the gap and discard the rest.

3. Design and implement new L&D programs that help your people build both technical skills—often referred to as hard skills—and

people skills—the famous *soft* skills—necessary to live up to the challenges coming their way. Make sure the capabilities and content of these programs have a clear link to the business needs. They can be reverse-engineered from the organization's business strategy.

4. Measure how well your organization applies the learning from L&D efforts and adjust these on an ongoing basis to make the most out of the resources you invest into closing the skill gap.

There are two different types of capabilities in the context of organizational identity, especially involved with strategy. The first type is knowledge and occupational skills that help you thrive in your field of expertise, known as hard skills. Look for the essentials that your people need to learn to deliver on their targets.

For many of us, 2020 was indicative of what it takes for a business to survive. Just out of necessity, many organizations jump-started or massively increased their digital transformation efforts. For millions of people, this meant becoming digitally savvy, practically overnight. For example, when the COVID-19 outbreak halted in-person gatherings, we had to rapidly shift face-to-face leadership development programs to online platforms. Delivering training and executive workshops online differs from delivering in-person sessions. To succeed, we had to acquire new capabilities.

The second type of capabilities are interpersonal skills—or people skills—to build and maintain successful relationships. They are vital for leaders and are therefore also referred to as leadership skills. Examples include being inspirational, being a people developer, using a coaching approach, and being a strategic system thinker. Subsets of these capabilities, however, are equally important for individual contributors, for example, skills related to negotiating win–win situations for sustainable success.

Just imagine a brilliant subject matter expert who is an excellent source of knowledge. Unfortunately, she has poor communication skills and doesn't care about helping colleagues with less experience learn and accomplish specific tasks. It is unlikely that this person would be successful in the long run. People skills are complementary to hard skills. We need both. We all have met colleagues whose hard skills were amazing but who also lacked people skills. Unfortunately, when those colleagues become leaders, they can make the lives of others miserable, sometimes without realizing it.

When it comes to leading strategy and change, there is no other group that is more critical to change than the leadership population of an organization, especially those in the middle. The top dogs typically are involved in strategy design and don't need to be sold on the value of a strategy and identity. They usually support implementation with everything they have. Time and again, I have seen leaders in the middle of an organization become distant to strategy and identity. I figured that the main reason is that leaders in the middle often don't know how to support it. They don't have enough information to engage their teams in a discussion. They dread questions from their people that they cannot answer, potentially making them look uninformed or weak.

A client once asked me, during a coffee break from a strategy design workshop, what I felt was the most crucial ingredient for a successful strategy rollout. As I thought the question was relevant to the whole team, we took it to the group. Interestingly enough, rather than arguing about projects, budgets, or other aspects of the strategy, the team agreed that developing the right set of strategy-related leadership capabilities was probably the most critical success factor in rolling out a plan.

They concluded that they could design the best possible strategy, but that many leaders in the organization lacked strategic acumen and the capability to inspire and drive change. The core team feared that a lack of strategy-related leadership capabilities would dilute their efforts. And boy, were they right. Sometime later, I caught up with the CEO, and he revealed that during the strategy design workshop, he realized that it wasn't only the middle management that lacked the necessary capabilities. Some members of the senior team struggled to lead the strategy rollout. He saw that the organization needed a different type of leadership with a new skill set to reach the next level of growth and maturity. As a result, he streamlined the organizational setup and built a new senior team, partly replacing incumbents with new hires.

The critical role of a leadership team can pose a bit of a challenge because they may stand too close to the operation. The less conscious or reflective a person is, the more they will reject the need for development.

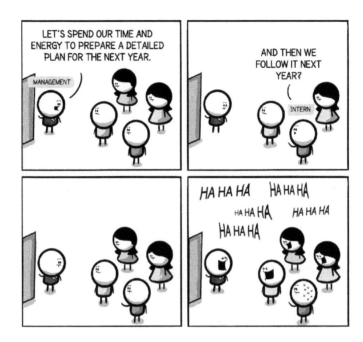

Some will even ridicule needed capabilities or a leadership-enabling program, not seeing how much they would benefit from such training. These individuals typically don't see that the capabilities that got them into a leadership seat can be different from the skills they now must develop to lead strategy and change.

As nutty as this may sound, I have come across managers who felt personally insulted when asked to attend a training program. These unteachable individuals typically comprise a fraction of an organization's population. But their negativity and cynicism can cause widespread harm. Funnily enough, when I was a rookie out of business school, I thought leaders climbed the organizational ladder mainly because of their leadership skills. In truth, other factors are more likely to define a leader's career trajectory, such as subject matter expertise, the ability to build networks, and promoting themselves. It also involves an innate drive to achieve status and financial success, and luck also plays a role—sometimes, it's chalked up to being at the right place at the right time.

On the bright side, I've found that most leaders typically see the need for capability development and are thankful for the opportunity. Fortunately, I have had the pleasure of working with companies explicitly looking for strategy and people skills when promoting talent. This makes a significant difference when strategy implementation is the name of the game. These organizations understand that designing a strategy is pointless if you are not willing to enable your leaders to implement it.

Develop and Empower Your Employees

When a client approached their new five-year customer support strategy, we invited a core team of senior leaders, representing thousands of employees worldwide. The leaders created a vision statement, packaged comprehensive workstreams, and realized that the changes they were about to trigger would massively challenge their people. This large-scale change would need a leadership population willing and able to drive implementation.

Senior leaders weren't too worried about the willingness but agreed that they needed to equip leaders with the necessary skills. They attributed such importance to the topic that the core team designed an entire workstream to bolster the plan. They placed it at the center of the logo depicting the new strategy and called it *Develop and Empower Our People*. Initially, this workstream produced a distinct program focused on building success-critical leadership capabilities.

The team wanted to equip every leader with the capabilities needed to lead change and implement the strategy in a transformational way. Not only did the program convey tools and methods, but it also provided reinforcing and anchoring elements, supporting participants to produce tangible results after completing the training. Within a few months, leaders in Europe, Asia, and North America went through the program, enabling them to transform the organization.

The training was focused on methods to activate teams for strategy implementation and beyond. Key content included how to explain a strategy without heavy jargon, translate strategy into individual targets, and hold people accountable for strategic change. In addition, participants combined rational and emotional communication methods to inspire action.

Identifying the ideal set of capabilities starts with focusing on the rationale behind an organization's identity or the business rationale of a strategy. The business rationale consists of strategic goals, like reaching new levels of customer satisfaction, revenues, or market share. From the business rationale, we derived performance outcomes that leaders would

produce. These outcomes can be a change in a condition, an achieve-
ment, a decrease or increase in something, or similar. From there, we
defined so-called moments that matter. These are scenarios in which
leaders perform in a desired way to produce a worthwhile performance
outcome. Figure 8.1 shows a real-life example of a strategy-related
high-performance learning journey.[3]

Business rationale	Performance outcomes	Moments-that-matter	Capabilities
• Increase the sales organization's contribution to success • Increase customer satisfaction and loyalty • Increase market share of our products and services • Increase revenues generated from service	• Increased strategic acumen: Every individual in the service org. can explain their contribution to the strategy • More tasks are aligned with the strategy • Sharpened focus and better resource allocation: Projects and initiatives contributing to the strategy are prioritized; non-contributing projects are re-evaluated • Workstream-related KPIs and strategic KPIs show desired development	• Leaders use every opportunity in day-to-day business to link projects, initiatives and tasks to the new strategy, in meetings, for their teams and themselves • Leaders discuss with teams and individuals how they contribute to the strategy, today and tomorrow • Leaders engage stakeholders in regions and countries and weave the new strategy into local strategies to secure implementation and impact • Leaders drive behavioral change necessary to enable change	• Understand importance of leading change and strategy in daily business • Know ways to engage key stakeholders inside and outside the organization to make strategy a topic, every day for everyone • Know how to run strategic dialog sessions with teams • Ability to explain the strategy in own words, without using jargon • Know how to make individual and team contribution to strategy visible • Know how to support, encourage, and hold people to account for strategic change

Figure 8.1 Client example of deriving strategic capabilities from a business rationale

It is not enough to train new capabilities. Research on training effectiveness shows that only 15 percent of participants successfully apply what they learn. The remaining 85 percent might try, fail, and stop—or don't try at all.[4] For long-term outcomes, prepare participants for training, help them identify day-to-day learning applications during the training, and provide support afterward.

Six Capabilities for Implementing Organizational Identity

Canada is famous for maple syrup, notable discoveries like penicillin, and life-changing inventions, such as the paint roller, basketball, and the Wonderbra—quite the list, eh? Another famous Canadian innovation was brought to the world by Mike Lazaridis: the BlackBerry, which dominated the pre-iPhone era; the success was built on technological ingenuity. As the age of buttonless smartphones began, Lazaridis refused to embrace change, staying strong-headed and loyal to his technology. As a result, Lazaridis almost ran the company into the ground.[5] He seemed to have lacked not one but several capabilities that led to BlackBerry's downfall, particularly strategic acumen and selflessness.

Staying on the topic of Canadian businesses, in 2018, I facilitated the offsite strategy meeting of a growth capital–backed software company called Tier1 Financial Solutions. Mark Notten and Phil Dias had been building the business from the ground up, and it was going strong. They knew it was the right time to update their strategy. The workshop triggered significant changes and developments over a couple of years that eventually led to a realization: Notten and Dias felt that they weren't the right ones for the job anymore. They saw that the business needed new leadership to tackle the next challenge of transforming the company into a software-as-a-service provider. As humble leaders, Notten and Dias displayed an outstanding level of selflessness and strategic acumen that helped them recognize the need of the business and the role they must play. They searched for their own replacements and stepped out of the way. A very different story to Mike Lazaridis, of Blackberry, and a very different legacy created. The example of Notten and Dias inspires us to lead beyond our egos, bringing about two strong spikes of the Legacy Trident: our legacies as people leaders and as creators of culture.

Self-aware managers show a combination of skills and character traits that make them exceptional. These traits and skills aren't innate; people can learn these capabilities. I have seen mediocre people managers leap to become truly inspiring personalities. It requires consciousness and willingness to become a better version of oneself, combining new skills and overcoming detrimental character traits (we all have them).

Specific skills enable one to lead through transformational change and leave a legacy to be proud of. As a senior leader, these are the power skills you should seek out when hiring talent. Some of the most relevant capabilities in the context of strategy and identity are these six:

Figure 8.2 The six capabilities for implementing organizational identity

Ability to Inspire

The ability to inspire enables leaders to influence others to embrace change by helping people discover what's in it for them. It is about engaging with people in a way that they feel your honest desire to help them succeed. It is about problem-solving creatively and working through differences on eye-level toward win–win outcomes.

Influencing is not about manipulating people into doing what you want them to or putting yourself into a favorable position at their cost. Winning while making others lose always backfires; people will eventually realize that you were tricking them, one way or another. They feel betrayed, and your leadership reputation would be tarnished. In contrast to manipulating, the term influencing inherently transports a positive connotation.

Ability to Collaborate

The ability to collaborate—with peers, leaders above or below you, and other stakeholders—is essential to develop and nurture relationships. It defines your network's reach, helping you expedite work. In a world where constant development is vital to the survival of organizations, creating an environment of connections, mutual respect, and support determines whether people grow to their full potential. Collaborative leaders intentionally delegate tasks to people, creating development opportunities, rather than getting rid of work by dumping it on someone's desk.

The ability to collaborate also means establishing a transparent feedback culture. In such a culture, people are encouraged to provide feedback in all directions: collaborating with their boss, peers, and other colleagues. Now, feedback is a loosely used term. I should mention that relaying feedback does not mean criticizing or diminishing someone's work. Feedback is based on the intention to help someone grow. It's conducive to avoid black-and-white terms like *positive* or *negative*—these don't do proper feedback justice. Feedback isn't positive or negative; rather it is reinforcing or developmental.

Reinforcing feedback recognizes behaviors that align with an organization's principles and purpose, for example. By providing this feedback, an individual realizes that their behavior is seen and valued. They know they're on the right path, thus reinforcing these patterns.

Developmental feedback provides people with learning opportunities based on behaviors or work results that differ from previously agreed-upon expectations. This kind of feedback also contains feed-*forward*, based on how to perform in the future, according to defined standards. Both forms of feedback foster individual growth.

Ability to Communicate

The ability to communicate is about conveying messages using appropriate terminology and communication structure. It entails speaking with compassion and humility, especially when conveying uncomfortable messages. In times of transformation, this helps people accept inconvenient truths because they realize their leaders are with them in the same boat, instead of talking down to them.

Proper communication requires listening as much as conveying a message. Asking powerful questions and listening helps people discover opportunities and options, which is an essential coaching skill. I am not suggesting that every leader should become a fully trained coach; rather, they should be able to apply coaching tools in the appropriate circumstances. The power of coaching can unleash unprecedented levels of creativity and ownership in your organization, driving you toward vision and impact.

A final communication skill essential to creating an organizational identity in which people can prosper is more about avoiding a certain type of communication: gossip. Gossip happens when an often unconstrained conversation includes derogatory comments about persons, ideas, events, or other circumstances. Gossip is like a forest fire ignited to befoul someone or something. People gossip because they are envious, want attention, want to feel superior, or because they are unhappy or angry about a decision or situation. They spread rumors, hear-say, or plain lies, and feed the flames. Years ago, I read a sentence that ingrained itself into my brain: *People who gossip with you also gossip about you.* We should not only stop engaging in gossip, but react appropriately, using sentences like "I realize you talk about Frank a lot. I was wondering why he interests you so much?" or "I don't appreciate listening to judgments about people unless we find a way to help them," or simply say "I am more interested in what you are up to." Such firm responses will stop the gossip.

Strategic Acumen

As far as I know, only a few characteristics distinguish humans from animals. The one I find the most intriguing is our ability to imagine the future and ourselves in it. Strategic acumen enables us to progress toward the future we want. It's the ability to think and act intentionally, based on a solid understanding of how a given organization operates within market dynamics. Strategic acumen includes the ability to detach oneself from daily operations and reimagine an area of responsibility; design what it should become, based on one's comprehension of and contribution to the total (business) value chain.

Like any other capability, strategic acumen isn't heaven-sent, but a skill we can acquire. It includes being perceptive, creative, future-oriented, and proactive, and developing a sense of confidence in one's judgment, resulting in taking decisions and calculated risks based on evidence and a sense of intuition. People with strong strategic acumen keep the bigger picture in mind when making seemingly smaller decisions, because they understand how they affect success on a larger scale. Before making a decision, the strategically savvy walk in different shoes and shed light on an issue from various perspectives, weighing the pros and cons.

In Chapter 3, we discussed foresight as a tool for strategic exploration and decision making. While you might not be doing all the research, data mining, and scenario development, you can still train yourself to become more future-savvy. Educate yourself on megatrends and their potential influence on your business. Become a futurist and train your mind to build bridges between seemingly unrelated topics. It's fun! Strategically savvy leaders can create foresight, build strategy, and help organizations turn strategy into quantifiable action and individual targets.

Leading by Intention

Being intentional is the antidote to being busy. At any given moment, there are different interest groups competing for your attention. It can be darn difficult to stay on top of things. A single moment of unintentional behavior can get you stuck in a useless meeting, screwing your agenda for the day. As much as you cannot spend a dollar twice, you cannot relive a minute. Therefore, leaders need to be intentional about how they best allocate their attention. Leading by intention requires prioritizing tasks, understanding the difference between an important and urgent issue, and managing attention.

Leading by intention goes beyond using time in the best possible way. In the context of organizational identity, leaders should be possibility-oriented and work toward solutions rather than just pointing out problems, objections, or reasons why something won't work. Intentional leadership is also related to the abilities mentioned earlier to communicate, collaborate, and inspire: it needs intentional messages, eye-level conversations, and a performance-oriented feedback culture to implement organizational identity.

Being intentional requires time to reflect, to be mindful, and to become aware. Therefore, leaders need to remove any barriers stopping them from leading by intention. Practice intention by removing time-wasting tasks, outdated processes, and cumbersome structures from your organization. Scrutinizing the status quo is intentional.

Selflessness

Selflessness is a character trait more than a skill, and we can learn how to be selfless. Selfless leaders don't highlight their own contributions. Instead, they seek opportunities to celebrate their teams' achievements and to champion others.

Building selflessness starts with understanding one's ego patterns. The ego will stand in the way of becoming a selfless leader. Instead of promoting others for exemplary behavior or outstanding performance, ego-driven leaders will search for their own recognition. Their ambition and drive will impede efforts of developing deep interpersonal connections and elevating the team above themselves. Creating awareness about ego patterns and learning how to keep one's selfish behavior in check is a good start to becoming a more selfless individual.

If you feel like your new strategy shouldn't require a lot of change and new capabilities, it is likely not worth the paper it is written on. If you are frowning right now, imagining, or even worrying about the cost involved for the development programs featuring these six essential capabilities, let me help you take a different perspective. Imagine the cost of not taking action. Imagine your company had invested months into designing a future-oriented strategy. You populated workstreams and communicated the new strategy to your staff—and then, you didn't equip them with the skills to bring it to life, and have tenure. Imagine the cost of failure to implement your strategy and what it would mean for the organization's competitiveness years down the road. There would likely be more than a few consequences for the organization's people.

A family-owned company I consulted on a new business strategy struggled to merge strategy and capability building. After thoroughly describing the connection between strategy and capability building, the management board bought into the concept. It felt like the organization was ready to intertwine strategy and leadership capability building into a powerful combination. It left me even more puzzled when I learned about their decision to roll out the new strategy while sticking to their already existing leadership development program. It was unclear how the capabilities of the training program would support leaders in implementing the new plan. Still, the board felt that tweaking the existing program would do the job.

Later, I learned from the chief HR officer that it was a short-term budgetary decision that contrasted the long-term nature of the strategy. As a result, strategy and leadership training remained separate buckets. While strategy became the task for business unit managers, leadership training—detached from their plan—remained a generic HR topic. This is not about being judgmental; putting oneself into the shoes of a company owner, juggling a bagful of different investment needs, it was a comprehensible decision. But also a missed opportunity.

CHAPTER 9

Form Follows Function

Avoiding the Symphony
of Destruction

In the late 19th and early 20th centuries, American architect Louis H. Sullivan established the theory that the design of a building should be derived from its purpose. It has further been developed into the principle *form follows function*[1] that has since been applied in fields from architecture and product design to software engineering.

In the context of organizational identity, *form follows function* is related to redesigning an organization's structures and processes to support identity and strategy. Structural changes might include selling off a business unit, changing the size of the board of directors, or cutting out an entire leadership level. It could also mean you create a new department or outsource noncore activities to external service providers. Even if your new identity does not require structural changes, it will potentially trigger a degree of process re-engineering, for example, to service customers in better ways, or to deploy a new collaboration model.

Let's assume you have aligned your leadership development efforts with the strategic needs of the business. You've trained the leadership population on capabilities and filled any skill gaps. As a result, leadership throughout the organization facilitates dialogs with their teams, creating quite a buzz. People start to understand the new identity, what their contribution will be, and discuss ways to reach their targets. Leaders even manage to help their teams realize what's in it for them emotionally and how they will personally benefit from a new strategy. You've done everything you could to get your organizational identity airborne. Will it fly?

Yes, if you can balance the factors that prevent your identity airplane from getting off the ground. A plane needs thrust, to accelerate to its takeoff speed. The fuel that fires its engine is your strategy, vision, and impact, and the positive attitudes toward the changes ahead. Drag pulls in the opposite direction of thrust and prevents the plane from reaching its desired speed. Gossip, cynicism, fear, and unfavorable market or economic conditions create the drag, to name a few. Some of these you can overcome, others are a given.

Then there is the lift: the factors that promote your identity. These include opinions from influential stakeholders whom people trust, dedicated project teams, PMOs, and governance boards that move the initiative forward. And, of course, leaders and individual contributors with the right capabilities will help steer the course.

Enough thrust, reduced drag, and all the lift you can create still won't do the job if you don't get rid of gravity. There's no getting rid of gravity, but you can reduce the weight of the plane. So, let's throw some stuff overboard that won't help your new identity fly—start with throwing out obsolete management systems.

Management Systems: The Frameworks of Your Organization

Management systems are the processes and structures that help steer an organization. If you are leading a small company, the only management system might be a simple set of guidelines for collaboration, put in place by you, the owner. In medium-sized organizations, management systems include many more policies; you might have a code of conduct in place, purchasing guidelines, and talent management routines. If you find yourself somewhere in a large enterprise, maybe even in a highly regulated environment, the odds are that they've captured nearly all aspects of business practices in some management system.

A standout example would be your newly established PMO to track the implementation of the strategy. The related controlling, reporting, and decision-making structure is a management system on its own. It helps you keep track of your efforts and guarantees that leaders can adjust the course of strategy execution when needed.

An identity process is a great opportunity to review management systems and assess whether they are still helpful. In HR, management systems need to mirror the implications of identity to make HR a true partner of the business. From identifying and attracting the right talent, to developing necessary hard and soft skills, and managing performance in line with the organization's values and purpose: without anchoring strategy and identity within HR management systems, the HR function likely will come up short of living up to the organization's expectations.

From being a driving force behind leadership principles and the desired leadership culture to aligning incentive and remuneration structures, the need to re-engineer management systems into enablers of identity is obvious. You don't want to force people into a situation where they need to decide whether they act according to new behavioral guidelines or whether they would rather maximize their year-end bonus. If incentive and remuneration systems continue to support previously accepted behaviors, people will likely do what's best for them financially to provide for their families.

In marketing, your identity should inform purpose-driven brand building, advertising, and PR, for example. If your marketing department continues to report on click rates of social media ads rather than channeling efforts into identity-supporting campaigns, something is off. Center your marketing efforts around your desired impact and the values that guide you.

Client relations are another area where management systems need to reflect your identity. Here, you can prove your seriousness about living up to your identity. A business I worked with had about a dozen clients. Losing one of them would significantly impact their financial performance. After that company had redefined its organizational identity, it set expectations for its employees and clients. They found that one client seemed to violate the new set of values through their business practices. The sales representatives of that client used all the dirty tricks in the book: from manipulating people emotionally to pressuring individuals into buying.

The company admitted to themselves that they couldn't see a way to change this client's business practices, as the senior management seemed to accept these behaviors. As a result, the company pulled the plug and didn't prolong its year-on-year contract with the client. Ensure your management systems are aligned to cater to the clientele you wish to sell to. It's about putting your money where your mouth is.

The larger your organization, the more difficult and time-consuming it will be to adjust management systems. Unfortunately, there is no way around it if you want to help your identity take off. Remember that management systems are typically not designed to support change but to support stable operations and the status quo. Therefore, adjusting these systems fast becomes all the more important, to remove weight and get airborne.

Governance and Staffing

Strong governance involves making trustworthy decisions in a space where people are ready to hear uncomfortable truths and engage in positive conflict to find the best way forward. Businesses that fail to create this type of environment avoid conflicts, and let the consequences poison an entire organization.

The fallout pits people against each other, making them suffer under ambiguity and a lack of decision making. One way or another, eventually decisions are being taken, sometimes in secret. If people don't understand the process and criteria used to arrive at a conclusion, they feel they depend on someone's mercy, which leaves them psychologically unsafe.

Transparent decision making goes a long way to building trust with individuals and teams. In Chapter 6, discussing strategy review sessions, I described the value of regularly checking the validity of what you aim to achieve. Now, who leads these different review and implementation sessions, and which individuals should sit on the related governance bodies, such as strategy boards?

Let's break this down to determine which approach makes the most sense for your business. The complexity and structure of your business will play an important role when installing a governing body. The approach I will describe is a tested method based on projects with for-profit multinationals. You can adjust it to your business size.

Core team members driving the design process usually take over responsibilities while implementing their new identity. They develop agency, take ownership, and want to see the dream come alive. They might lead a workstream or a strategic project within a workstream, serve on a strategy review board, or support the initiative through presentations and speeches during the rollout phase. They become change champions, agents, and ambassadors.

Apart from core team members, there are likely some other bright minds in your organization whom you should think to involve. This is a chance to provide some high potentials with growth opportunities, exposing them to work related to strategy and identity. In addition to their subject matter expertise and leadership experience, you can help them round out their portfolios to become more valuable contributors over time.

Serving on a governance body related to strategy and identity is often seen as an opportunity and honor. Involving a broader number of people to represent different parts of the organization will help you spread the word and make strategy and identity a hot topic. People will start talking about strategy and change with colleagues. And by spreading the work over additional shoulders, you avoid overburdening your most valuable resources.

Implementation Board

Three different bodies help keep the momentum and implementation on track. The implementation board is the first body to install. As the name suggests, this board will be integral in steering the unveiling of your new identity. It is the conductor, artfully coordinating the different forces and ensuring they develop into a beautifully orchestrated image.

The implementation board secures the operationalization of your identity: they track the strategy rollout and oversee that purpose and principles find their way into the day-to-day. To avoid falling back into previous patterns, they urge the organization to follow through on capability building and adjusting management systems.

The implementation board typically consists of those leading the rollout of elements of your identity, including your strategic workstream leaders and leaders of purpose- and principle-related projects. In addition, C-level executives and board directors contribute experience, secure focus, and help steer the discussion.

Internal and external facilitators can help you structure these meetings, especially at the start of a rollout phase. Teams that are less strategically versed will benefit from having a neutral perspective in the room, aiming for the best possible result, and supporting the team to become functional and address potentially difficult discussions.

The implementation board is seeking to understand if the strategic workstreams are on track, or if there are any barriers they can eliminate. The board can adjust resources, expectations, and focus on helping initiatives gain traction; they also make sure workstreams don't duplicate structures, and instead learn from each other.

During these meetings, initiative leaders report on the implementation status, highlighting milestones achieved, identified barriers, or areas in need of support. They will likely raise questions, while addressing requirements toward adjacent initiatives or leadership. They engage in solution-oriented conversations that support the identity rollout.

Bringing balance to the discussions while allowing an intense exchange of arguments is crucial. Initiative leaders are typically passionate about their projects. While pushing for implementation and fighting for success, they sometimes forget that their initiative is part of a bigger picture. The discussions should promote collaboration between initiatives.

A client of mine nimbly aligned around mission, values, and collaboration guidelines. Later, the team also created a vision, a strategic KPI dashboard, and the workstreams that should drive those KPIs in the right direction. The smooth process up until this point resulted in high expectations regarding the speed of execution and results.

Only when the implementation started did some individuals on the implementation board figure out that they depended heavily on input that they awaited from outside their business unit. Receiving the information took longer than initially expected and delayed timelines.

As a result, people became frustrated over the slower-than-expected progress. They didn't want to accept any further delay and engaged in a discussion about reallocating resources from one workstream to another, hoping this would solve the issue. All workstreams were running at full speed at this point. No one was overly keen on slowing their teams down, as they feared a loss of momentum and a drop in morale.

Only through honest and unguarded discussions did the implementation board come up with an alternative approach that brought success. The argument was heated, but fair. Two workstream leaders committed to temporarily lending team members to help accelerate the department's most prominent workstream. Even if it certainly wasn't an easy decision, it was a necessary step in the overall progress.

A valuable learning for the implementation board was that no matter how much planning they invested into strategy design, execution doesn't follow a straight line. Resilience and agility are helpful traits to readjust the course promptly, while keeping the end goal in mind.

How often your identity implementation board meets will depend on your progress rate. At the start of your identity rollout, mainly when it entails a new business strategy, you'll want to meet in short intervals, to keep focus and urgency high, and to help the organization understand the importance of the initiative. Your goal is to create some positive buzz.

The earlier you achieve the first results, and even if it's *just some low-hanging fruit*, the earlier you can communicate success stories. These will propel your initiative further, create acceptance, and serve as a basis for more change. Once the implementation is well underway, and there is less and less need for adjusting, the implementation board would meet in longer intervals, eventually only every three to four months potentially.

Strategy Review Board

The second governance body you want to install is your strategy review board. While the implementation board oversees the efficient roll out of your initiative, the review board ensures the initiative remains effective and relevant.

The review board runs the strategy review sessions. By its nature, it has tremendous power and would typically consist of the same leaders and experts as in the design phase. These are the individuals who would know the most about any discussions, assumptions, or hypotheses that went into the strategy initially.

The review board benchmarks the existing strategy against the current environment and discusses the resulting implications. Consequently, they can decide on changes in scope and direction, shifts in resource allocation, or workstream continuity. Board decisions would find their way into the implementation process.

Project Management Office (PMO)

Let's talk about the workhorses of any identity initiative, your PMO, the third body. These are the people that provide structure, research, and other support. They design reports, discuss issues with project leaders, suggest resources and methods for decision making. Your PMO is the structural backbone of your initiative, and I cannot overstate the importance of establishing a reliable PMO. Staffing requires a good understanding of the specific role of the PMO in your context.

Depending on their experience, PMO managers can prepare and conduct meetings for the implementation board, the review board, and the board of directors. I have seen PMO leaders become facilitators of change and cherished contributors sitting on governance boards themselves.

Your PMO should complement the governance boards they support. In other words, if your boards mainly consist of creative libertines, use the PMO for providing structure, process, and follow-through. If your boards aren't short of process-oriented and fact-based members, throw some fresh thinking and new energy into the mix.

A PMO should be able to collaborate with external stakeholders as well, especially with management consultancies. When a client once staffed a strategy PMO with a new manager who had only recently joined the company, I was curious to meet the person. After we first met, I realized that we had quite different personality types.

As an external facilitator, my role is to help executives prepare and run governance board meetings, aligning content and flow with the PMO lead. I was curious how the collaboration would play out, and jokingly told the CEO that he couldn't have picked a better challenge for me, given how different we were. The CEO laughed and admitted that he had selected this PMO manager to balance the personalities in the initiative. He chose wisely. The PMO manager contributed to a strong rollout and became a valued member of the team.

A Management System to Prioritize Work

In theory, a new business strategy should free up resources because it is a framework to prioritize work and let go of everything that doesn't support it. In real life, it's not that simple. Often, organizations feel they need additional resources to bring strategy to life. Ask any business owner, leader, or key contributor how they're doing, and chances are high you'll get a response like "Overwhelmed!" or "Busy!" or even "Taking it day by day!" They're likely dismayed by the length of their to-do lists, or even just wondering if all the work they put in day after day is even getting them anywhere.

Some people's default is to duck and cover, keep their heads down, and hope for the storm to pass. Others search for productivity hacks to put even more work into an already crammed agenda.

Real productivity does not come in the form of some productivity training—because those tactics only work if you are intentional about what you do. You can outsource, delegate, or productivity hack yourself out of business if you don't solve the fundamental issues first. It starts with understanding the difference between intentional productivity and busy work.

A pattern I found across most businesses I worked with is that people feel overwhelmed when their priorities are watered down. If everything is important and urgent, nothing is. As a result, people stretch themselves too thin, and nothing gets the attention it requires.

Having 80 tasks on your priority to-do list is not a badge of honor. It's better to tear the whole list down and only add back on what is needed. By letting go of things that don't matter, you can avoid burnout, heart attacks, and stress-induced mental illnesses. Give yourself permission to let go by using your strategy initiative as a decision-making tool.

Empower your people to let go of busy work and free resources for what matters. If you are serious about your business, you can't afford to waste time with busy work. If it's not business-critical, stop doing it. Don't outsource or delegate it. Eliminate it instead. The tasks you keep should have a direct link to your individual targets, which were derived from the strategy. This is how you create intentional productivity.

A Cautionary Tale

Given that leaders sometimes move on, anchoring identity through management systems becomes even more crucial. If the head of your initiative moves up the ranks or pursues a new career outside the organization, one of two things will happen.

If you are lucky, the leader of the initiative was conscious enough to build a strong team around them. These people now continue the work until it's done. If you are unlucky—and I have seen this happen twice during my career—the whole initiative is dead in the water within no time. The leader leaves, and without their passion and focus attention fades, momentum slips, the initiative stalls, the organization reverts to old behaviors and practices.

When I worked with a tech multinational's German branch to shape the new identity of a division, things got tricky early on. The newly appointed director wanted to build a functional team, a clear-cut strategy, and a clearer value proposition. Starting the project, various individuals needed to come to terms with interpersonal issues in the past, others publicly displayed little interest in the process, and one individual mercilessly second-guessed every comment made by the director.

Admittedly a challenging environment to start such an endeavor. While interest in the initiative grew over time, people rallied around a strategy and started to address issues more openly. At some point, it felt like the team had actually tasted blood. From there, the tide shifted, and it seemed as if we were headed for success. However, the change was not yet anchored within the business area's management systems. Shortly after my involvement ended, when implementation was underway but still fragile—I received a call. The leader let me in on the decision that she was about to leave the organization.

Without her to passionately drive the implementation of the new identity, I feared that everything would eventually go up in flames. The only option I had was to trust the people involved and offer support. I called one of the more supportive colleagues to figure out how we could save the initiative. It was just to learn that the day the leader left the organization, everything had imploded. Without the leader holding the group together, old rivalries broke open again, and the team dropped the ball on their commitments.

Communication—The Magic Wand

Communication is the all-essential oil for an identity initiative. When a client had just completed a merger, they were shooting for the top spot in the market. While the physical aspects of the merger, such as housing and IT, went well, the cultural merger was dragging behind. The company struggled to overhaul work procedures and create a general work philosophy across all units. As a result, performance and morale were fading, and client satisfaction dropped. Leadership wanted to secure the expected synergies from the merger and decided to start an organizational identity initiative. They went all the way, from shaping new corporate values and rebrushing their strategy to building leadership capabilities.

We challenged leadership to increase their communication efforts and engage their teams in conversations about strategy and change at every possible opportunity. Senior leaders toured all sites, turning their strategy presentations into happenings, and addressing their audiences using appropriate terminology, with the right level of detail. The company monitored the progress of implementing organizational identity using focus groups, online surveys, and dedicated governance bodies.

According to companywide surveys and interviews, by going all in on communication, they broke through to their teams and established a

---

new organizational identity. It resulted in higher morale, increased performance, and rising customer satisfaction.

No one in their right mind would neglect the need for communication in the context of strategy and change. Every business I've ever worked with had a *communication issue*, according to people we interviewed at the start of a project. Blaming communication is a different way of describing that there is a lack of change leadership, and no change management system in place.

Organizations regularly cause significant damage by neglecting the need for such systems. There are various change management models, such as Kübler–Ross, Adkar, or McKinsey's 7S. Make sure you underpin your efforts accordingly, to secure successful follow-through. When it comes to leading change, let me point you in the direction of John Kotter's work. I won't discuss these models here, and instead focus on what they have in common: the importance of communication.

There Is No One-Size-Fits-All Approach for Communication

It may sound daunting, but it's not as simple as a math equation. Every organization is different and needs a dovetailed communication approach based on its general culture, current mood, expectations, and experience.

The culture of an organization is a tricky thing to grasp. Especially when you've been part of an organization for a longer period. It might be difficult to perceive and describe culture objectively when you've become a part of it yourself. It's not impossible though, especially when you are a keen observer. Over time, you see and hear things in the hallways, meeting rooms, or on the shop floor. You might notice behaviors are being tolerated—from being late to joking about a colleague.

There are some implications around culture depending on the type of organization you are leading. Imagine the different approaches, for example, regarding risk-taking or change readiness, when comparing a traditional, risk-averse *old economy* company and a venture capital-backed, hyper-growth startup.

As opposed to the general culture, the current mood of an organization characterizes how people within an organization feel at a certain moment in time. While a company can have a certain culture, for example, hierarchical with centralized decision making and slow to adopt change, its current mood can be very different. Mood may be triggered by external factors, or a sudden awareness that their business stands in flames. Panic and fear, as well as hopes and desires, have the power to influence an organization's mood strongly.

As a result, with a proper communication approach, leaders might be able to push for a level of change that would seem impossible in regular times. It goes back to those inflection points described in Chapter 5, external events that present great opportunities or threats and require a swift answer, like an unexpected change in an industry's regulatory environment.

Expectations and experience of an organization about strategy, change, and organizational identity should inform your communication approach as well. Analyze what types of communication worked well in the past, and why; you can build on these experiences. Also, there might be communication you should avoid to prevent overwhelming your people.

Are people expecting leadership to just lead, and they will follow, because they fully trust in their capabilities? Or do they want to have a say and take an active part in shaping identity? How can we engage them early on? How much communication, about what topics, will the organization expect, and need?

Communication Goes Both Ways—Establish a Dialog

Organizations are usually not democracies. Leadership decides, management executes—but making organizational identity a one-way road, a purely top-down led approach is certainly not helpful. Engage your organization early on, in meaningful two-way conversations about strategy, impact, and values. Listen to what people want to contribute and let them take an active role in workshops, focus groups, and surveys. Foster a participatory approach to designing the organizational identity.

It might slow down the design process in the beginning: more opinions, more problems. But once you've worked through the cacophony, a new organizational identity will stand on a broad and stable basis, as opposed to having created it in a smaller team, start to end—if you do that don't expect people to love what they see when you present the final product. Engage your people early, communicate, and listen. This will make your life way easier when you start rolling out a new identity. Ultimately, people are more likely to support a world that they cocreate.

For the client I mentioned that had just gone through a merger, a true test came when the company announced they would shut down a site, consolidating operations into one hub. Leadership expected that morale and productivity would plummet, when the opposite happened: employees showed understanding of the decision. They had internalized the company strategy through relentless communication. An unexpectedly high number of employees from the closing site applied for other jobs in the new hub, even if this meant moving halfway across the country. They said that their new identity had shown them what a great company it was, and that they wanted to continue working for it.

Part 3 Executive Summary

The Nine Elements of Organizational Identity

The support structures in those Cuban buildings held everything in place. In a similar way, you want to establish a solid scaffolding around your strategy and allow the organization's form to follow its function. The three elements discussed in Part 3 are the shield that will deflect potential wrecking balls aiming to tear your legacy down. Unless you want to sing the symphony of destruction, build the support structure with the same rigor that you used to formulate your strategy.

Questions to Explore

Targets

- Are leaders and individual contributors clear on their contribution to implementing your organizational identity?
- Can you link daily activities to strategy, values, and desired impact?
- Are individual targets measurable and specific?
- Do you focus on the 20 percent of measures, targets, and actions that make the 80 percent difference?
- Which guidelines and supporting documents are in place to help people understand what's expected of them?

Capabilities

- To what degree is your leadership population able to lead strategy and change?
- How well does your leadership development effort connect with your organizational identity and business rationale?
- Do your leadership training programs include the *Six Capabilities for Implementing Organizational Identity*?
- Are programs in place to enable individual contributors to perform according to new standards and ways of working?
- Does everyone embrace what's in it for them?

Management Systems

- Is there a system of accountability in place for leaders to promote organizational identity?

- Did you install the necessary governance bodies to support the implementation process?
- Is your PMO a strong partner to governance boards, complementing their skills?
- Did all functions of your organization align their practices with the new identity?
- What is your plan to overcommunicate organizational identity?

Epilogue

Strategy changes, identity endures. Identity is the stabilizer that keeps your business afloat when strategic change brings about rough waters. When leaders combine commercial and cultural aspects, they tap into the hidden power of strategy. They become drivers of commercial success and leave a mark: a legacy of significance. To achieve this, leaders must deploy people-centric strategies, supported by capability-building and management systems.

Strategy is a topic for everyone in an organization. Embedding strategy within the Nine Elements of Organizational Identity unleashes the energy your organization needs to thrive in the marketplace. Rallying your people around impact, values, and strategy becomes your secret sauce. It sets you apart from competitors who don't consider much other than being profitable. Strategy alone is not sustainable as it can easily be copied and pasted. By contrast, an organization built on the Nine Elements of Organizational Identity is unique and creates a lasting competitive advantage.

Some key takeaways and actionable items:

- *Uncover your moral compass*: formulate what you stand for as a human being.
- *Dig for the diamond values*: personally, and as an organization, become aware of what you truly value and how it informs behaviors.
- *Visualize your living legacy*: get to the core of what *success* and *significance* mean to you.
- *Define the higher purpose and desired impact*: explore it for yourself first. Then find or build an organization that helps you produce that impact.
- *Explore how you can do the right thing*: you can do the right thing while also being financially successful: do good while doing well.

- *Distill your mission*: be clear about what your organization does, and for whom.
- *Create a balanced vision*: infuse heart and brain, detail and aspiration, purpose and measurability, and compile a KPI dashboard to track your progress.
- *Formulate clear workstreams*: make sure your workstreams influence strategic KPIs and set SMART goals.
- *Derive individual targets*: break down goals into individual contributions to move strategy and identity into action.
- *Link capability development to organizational identity*: enable leaders to drive implementation and empower people to contribute.
- *Adjust management systems*: support your change efforts through processes and structures that accelerate identity implementation.
- *Use the legacy trident*: regularly reflect on your living legacy toward the people you lead, the business you represent, and society.

I encourage you to visit my website to access the many supporting resources mentioned in the book. These include worksheets, templates, guidelines, questionnaires, specific exercises, and strategy online courses. These resources were pressure tested in client projects and make a difference when cohesively defining and implementing strategy and identity in your workplace.

> **To access the field guide, visit https://brueckmann.ca/fieldguide**

I invite you to contribute your reactions, suggestions, viewpoints, and experiences, the good, the bad, and the ugly. Send me your successes, failures, and questions when applying the tools and concepts from this book.

You are ready to design organizational identity. Be fearless and conscious in your endeavors—enjoy the ride!

Notes

Chapter 1

1. "Our Core Values—Patagonia" (2022).
2. McIntyre (2021).
3. "Our Mission" (2021).
4. Kantabutra and Avery (2010), pp. 37–45.
5. Wales (2022).
6. Kaplan and Norton (2004).

Chapter 2

1. Cain, Lipton, Rosenblum, and Savitt (2020).
2. Malnight, Buche, and Dhanaraj (2019).
3. Henderson (2015), pp. 22–47.
4. Arnold (2020).
5. Chouinard (2022).

Chapter 3

1. Brueckmann (2023).
2. Reeves, Haanaes, and Sinha (2016).
3. Easterly (2021).
4. "Did Peter Drucker Say That?" (2022).
5. Clifton (2022).

Part 2

1. Ollhoff (2007).

Chapter 4

1. Grant (2021).
2. Conscious Leadership Group and Franks (2014).

3. Gordon-Levitt (2019).
4. Doz (2018).

Chapter 5

1. Grove (1999).
2. Kenny (2021).
3. Steare, Fitt, and Bulmer (2013).
4. Barsade and O'Neill (2014), pp. 551–598.
5. "Code of Conduct" (2022).

Chapter 6

1. "Our Growth Pillars" (2020).
2. Kantabura and Avery (2010), pp. 37–45.
3. Kanter (2014).
4. Knight (2018).
5. Sanger and Wales (2022).
6. Heath and Heath (2010).
7. Simon (2021).
8. Oberholzer-Gee (2021).

Part 3

1. Kotter, Rathgeber, and Mueller (2006).

Chapter 7

1. "Ethics and Integrity" (2022).

Chapter 8

1. Segel and Blessing (2021).
2. Agrawal, De Smet, Poplawski, and Reich (2021).
3. Brinkerhoff, Apking, and Boon (2019).

4. Kirkpatrick and Kirkpatrick (2016).
5. Gustin (2013).

Chapter 9

1. Leslie (2010), pp. 83–93.

References

"Code of Conduct." 2022. Morgan Stanley. www.morganstanley.com/about-us-governance/code-of-conduct.

"Did Peter Drucker Say That?" 2022. Drucker Institute. www.drucker.institute/did-peter-drucker-say-that/.

"Ethics and Integrity." July 23, 2022. Roche Canada. F. Hoffmann-La Roche Ltd. www.rochecanada.com/en/about-roche/ethics-and-integrity.html#:~:text=The%20Roche%20Group%20Code%20of%20Conduct&text=It%20contains%20guidance%20in%20the,business%20and%20comprehensive%20compliance%20management.

"Our Core Values—Patagonia." 2022. Patagonia Outdoor Clothing & Gear. www.patagonia.com/core-values/.

"Our Growth Pillars." 2020. McDonald's. https://corporate.mcdonalds.com/corpmcd/about-us/our-growth-strategy.html.

"Our Mission." May 7, 2021. Sea Shepherd Global. www.seashepherdglobal.org/who-we-are/our-mission.

Agrawal, S., A. De Smet, P. Poplawski, and A. Reich. March 1, 2021. "Beyond Hiring: How Companies Are Reskilling to Address Talent Gaps." McKinsey & Company. www.mckinsey.com/capabilities/people-and-organizational-performance/our-insights/beyond-hiring-how-companies-are-reskilling-to-address-talent-gaps.

Arnold, P. January 30, 2020. "Roche Says Closed Chinese Cities Hinder Virus Diagnostics Test Deliveries." *Reuters*. Thomson Reuters. www.reuters.com/article/us-china-health-swiss-roche-idUSKBN1ZT14L.

Barsade, S. and O. O'Neill. 2014. "What's Love Got to Do With It? A Longitudinal Study of the Culture of Companionate Love and Employee and Client Outcomes in a Long-Term Care Setting." *Administrative Science Quarterly* 59, no. 4, pp. 551–598. https://doi.org/10.1177/0001839214538636.

Brinkerhoff, R., A. Apking, and E. Boon. 2019. *Improving Performance Through Learning: A Practical Guide for Designing High Performance Learning Journeys*. Columbia, SC.

Brueckmann, A. 2023. *Secrets of Next Level Entrepreneurs*. John Wiley.

Cain, K., M. Lipton, S. Rosenblum, and W. Savitt. May 27, 2020. *On the Purpose of the Corporation*. The Harvard Law School Forum on Corporate Governance. https://corpgov.law.harvard.edu/2020/05/27/on-the-purpose-of-the-corporation/#:~:text=The%20purpose%20of%20a%20corporation,and%20communities)%2C%20as%20determined%20by.

Chouinard, Y. September 14, 2022. *A Letter From Yvon Chouinard.* Patagonia. www.patagonia.ca/stories/a-letter-from-yvon-chouinard/story-127258.html.

Clifton, J. October 4, 2022. *Does Capitalism Need a Soul Transplant?* Gallup. www.gallup.com/workplace/347156/capitalism-need-soul-transplant.aspx.

Conscious Leadership Group and Franks, G. 2014. "Locating Yourself." *The Conscious Leadership Group, LLC.* www.conscious.is/.

Doz, Y. June 1, 2018. "The Strategic Decisions That Caused Nokia's Failure." *INSEAD Knowledge.* https://knowledge.insead.edu/strategy/strategic-decisions-caused-nokias-failure.

Easterly, J. July 6, 2021. *Leadership Lessons From the Pandemic.* LinkedIn. www.linkedin.com/pulse/leadership-lessons-from-pandemic-jen-easterly/.

Gordon-Levitt, J. February 24, 2019. *Joseph Gordon-Levitt on How Craving Attention Makes You Less Creative.* TED. www.ted.com/talks/joseph_gordon_levitt_how_craving_attention_makes_you_less_creative.

Grant, A. 2021. *Think Again: The Power of Knowing What You Don't Know.* Random House Large Print.

Grove, A. 1999. *Only the Paranoid Survive: How to Exploit the Crisis Points That Challenge Every Company.* New York, NY: Currency Doubleday.

Gustin, S. September 24, 2013. "The Fatal Mistake That Doomed BlackBerry." *Time.* https://business.time.com/2013/09/24/the-fatal-mistake-that-doomed-blackberry/.

Heath, C. and D. Heath. 2010. *Made to Stick—Why Some Ideas Survive and Others Die.* New York, NY: Random House.

Henderson, R. 2015. "Making the Business Case for Environmental Sustainability." *Leading Sustainable Change,* pp. 22–47. https://doi.org/10.1093/acprof:oso/9780198704072.003.0002.

Kantabutra, S. and G. Avery. 2010. "The Power of Vision: Statements That Resonate." *Journal of Business Strategy* 31, no. 1, pp. 37–45. https://doi.org/10.1108/02756661011012769.

Kanter, R.M. August 1, 2014. "A Vision Is Not Just a Picture of What Could Be; It Is an Appeal to Our Better Selves, a Call to Become Something More." Twitter. https://twitter.com/rosabethkanter/status/495302569405976576.

Kaplan, R. and D. Norton. 2004. *Strategy Maps: Converting Intangible Assets Into Tangible Outcomes.* Boston, MA: Harvard Business School Press.

Kenny, G. September 17, 2021. "Your Company's Purpose Is Not Its Vision, Mission, or Values." *Harvard Business Review.* https://hbr.org/2014/09/your-companys-purpose-is-not-its-vision-mission-or-values.

Kirkpatrick, J. and W.K. Kirkpatrick. 2016. *Kirkpatrick's Four Levels of Training Evaluation.* Alexandria, VA: ATD Press.

Knight, P. 2018. *Shoe Dog: A Memoir by the Creator of Nike.* London, UK: Simon & Schuster.

Kotter, J., H. Rathgeber, and P. Mueller. 2006. *Our Iceberg Is Melting: Changing and Succeeding Under Any Conditions*. United States: Portfolio.

Leslie, T. 2010. "Dankmar Adler's Response to Louis Sullivan's 'the Tall Office Building Artistically Considered': Architecture and the 'Four Causes.'" *Journal of Architectural Education* 64, no. 1, pp. 83–93. https://doi.org/10.1111/j.1531-314x.2010.01102.x.

Malnight, T.W., I. Buche, and C. Dhanaraj. August 27, 2019. "Put Purpose at the Core of Your Strategy." *Harvard Business Review*. https://hbr.org/2019/09/put-purpose-at-the-core-of-your-strategy.

McIntyre, G. June 29, 2021. "With Heat Warnings in Effect, B.C. Businesses Take Measures to Protect Employees and Customers." *Vancouver Sun*. https://vancouversun.com/news/local-news/with-heat-warnings-in-effect-businesses-take-measures-to-protect-employees-and-customers.

Oberholzer-Gee, F. 2021. *Better, Simpler Strategy: A Value-Based Guide to Exceptional Performance*. Boston, MA: Harvard Business Review Press.

Ollhoff, J. 2007. *Strategy 101: An Introduction and Guide*. Farmington, MN: Sparrow Media Group.

Reeves, M., K. Haanaes, and J. Sinha. 2016. *Your Strategy Needs a Strategy: How to Choose and Execute the Right Approach*. New York, NY: Summaries.com.

Sanger, L. and J. Wales. October 3, 2022. *Purpose*. Wikimedia Foundation. https://en.wikipedia.org/wiki/Wikipedia:Purpose.

Segel, H.L. and K. Blessing. October 14, 2021. *The Capability-Building Imperative: Make "Purposeful Investments" in People*. McKinsey & Company. www.mckinsey.com/capabilities/people-and-organizational-performance/our-insights/the-capability-building-imperative-make-purposeful-investments-in-people.

Simon, H. 2021. *True Profit!: No Company Ever Went Broke Turning a Profit*. Cham, Switzerland: Copernicus Books.

Steare, R., J. Fitt, and T. Bulmer. 2013. *Ethicability: How to Decide What's Right and Find the Courage to Do It*. London: Roger Steare Consulting Limited.

Wales, J. November 16, 2022. *Prime Objective*. Wikimedia Foundation. https://en.wikipedia.org/wiki/Wikipedia:Prime_objective.

Illustrations and Figures

All illustrations and figures created by the author, except:

Figure 4.1 "Locating yourself," by Conscious Leadership Group and Graeme Franks.

All cartoons copyright by workchronicles.com, all rights reserved.

About the Author

A strategy practitioner with over 20 years of business experience, **Alex Brueckmann** is the founder and CEO of Brueckmann Executive Consulting based in Vancouver, Canada. His clients include executive teams and CEOs looking to achieve greater strategic clarity. As a facilitator, speaker, and author, he helps businesses reach unmatched levels of alignment, performance, and results. Alex has been praised for his honest ways of bringing actionable strategy advice to entrepreneurs and executives.

An entrepreneur himself, Alex built and scaled businesses in Europe and North America. For the varying needs of his clients, he offers a range of online courses, workshops, and consulting packages.

Alex holds a B.Sc. in General Management from European Business School (EBS) in Germany, as well as certifications from Harvard Business School and INSEAD.

Join Alex's LinkedIn community, enjoy his newsletter *Building Bridges,* and benefit from strategy online courses on **brueckmann.ca**.

For speaking and consulting inquiries, please use the contact form on the website or e-mail Alex's team at **alex@brueckmann.ca**.

Also Available By Alex Brueckmann

Drawing on the secrets of some of the brightest minds in entrepreneurship, *Secrets of Next Level Entrepreneurs* is an indispensable guide to thriving in business and leading a balanced life. It is a book of actionable solutions you can put into practice right away—written by business owners and leaders for business owners and leaders.

Alex Brueckmann has collected strategies and tactics from some of the most talented leaders on the planet to help you future-proof your business by learning essential skills, understanding yourself, and shifting your mindset accordingly.

Next level entrepreneurs build profitable businesses that contribute to more equitable communities, social and environmental justice, and a

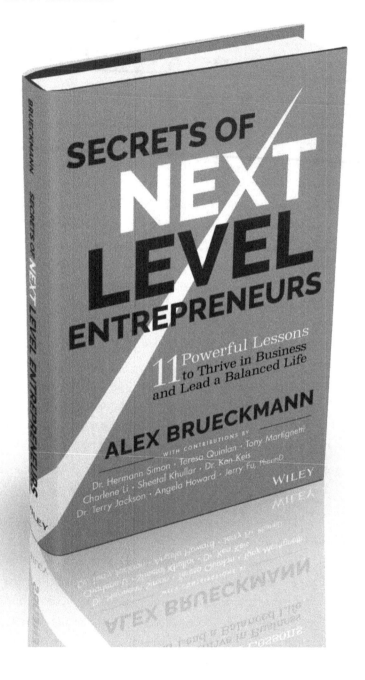

world that is worth living in for us, our children, and the generations to come.

In this book, you learn the three mission-critical pillars that contribute to building future-proof businesses—strategy, leadership, and self-care:

- How to create a winning business strategy
- How to boost your profits through clever pricing
- How to create value and a sustainable impact
- How to master disruption
- How to build a high-performance culture
- How to create an impact culture
- How to make conflict resolution easier
- How to self-lead in challenging times
- How to create a balanced life
- How to transform yourself through self-awareness
- How to adopt four powerful mindsets to conquer love, overcome death, and succeed in business

Secrets of Next Level Entrepreneurs is available as audiobook, hardcover, and e-book.

Index

OTHER TITLES IN THE STRATEGIC MANAGEMENT COLLECTION

John Pearce, Villanova University, Editor

- *Global Business Strategy* by Cornelis A. de Kluyver and John A. Pearce II
- *Sustaining High Performance in Business* by Jeffrey S. Harrison
- *How to Navigate Strategic Alliances and Joint Ventures* by Meeta Dasgupta
- *Strategic Engagement* by Christopher Crosby
- *Business Strategy in the Artificial Intelligence Economy* by J. Mark Munoz and Al Naqvi
- *Strategic Organizational Alignment* by Chris Crosby
- *First and Fast* by Stuart Cross
- *Strategies for University Management* by J. Mark Munoz and Neal King
- *Strategies for University Management, Volume II* by J. Mark Munoz and Neal King
- *Strategic Management* by Cornelius A. de Kluyver and John A. Pearce
- *Strategic Management* by Linda L. Brennan and Faye Sisk
- *Strategic Management of Healthcare Organizations* by Jeffrey S. Harrison and Steven M. Thompson
- *Developing Successful Business Strategies* by Rob Reider

Concise and Applied Business Books

The Collection listed above is one of 30 business subject collections that Business Expert Press has grown to make BEP a premiere publisher of print and digital books. Our concise and applied books are for...

- Professionals and Practitioners
- Faculty who adopt our books for courses
- Librarians who know that BEP's Digital Libraries are a unique way to offer students ebooks to download, not restricted with any digital rights management
- Executive Training Course Leaders
- Business Seminar Organizers

Business Expert Press books are for anyone who needs to dig deeper on business ideas, goals, and solutions to everyday problems. Whether one print book, one ebook, or buying a digital library of 110 ebooks, we remain the affordable and smart way to be business smart. For more information, please visit www.businessexpertpress.com, or contact sales@businessexpertpress.com.

Printed in the USA
CPSIA information can be obtained
at www.ICGtesting.com
LVHW021401261023
762144LV00023B/96/J